A

'The development of Alpha courses has been one of the most significant areas of growth during the Decade of Evangelism. Now that tens of thousands of people have completed these courses many are asking "What next?" I warmly commend this book as an answer to that question.'

George Carey
Archbishop of Canterbury

'Many churches which have benefited greatly from running Alpha courses, have been faced with the question "What now?". Michael Green's book offers an answer – a readable resource that builds on the strengths of Alpha while drawing people deeper into the life of discipleship.'

David Hope
Archbishop of York

'When I was a young Christian, Michael's books helped me enormously with his customary clarity and warmth of conviction. I am sure this new book will be immensely helpful for many who have recently completed an Alpha course.'

Rob Warner
Queen's Road Baptist Church, Wimbledon

'*After Alpha* answers so many questions from those who have recently put their trust in Christ, and from others whose faith has been revived, but who are asking "What now?". It is highly recommended for those who want to be useful and find fulfilment in developing their commitment to the greatest story ever told.'

Gerald Coates
Pioneer

'A great book for growing churches, which will sustain and encourage the current renewal in Christian confidence. Packed full of wisdom and insight.'

Alister McGrath
Principal, Wycliffe Hall, Oxford

By the same author

After Alpha

MICHAEL GREEN

KINGSWAY PUBLICATIONS
EASTBOURNE

Text illustrations by Taffy Davies

First published 1998
Reprinted 1998
This new edition 2001

ISBN 1 84291 024 8

Published by
KINGSWAY PUBLICATIONS
Lottbridge Drove, Eastbourne, BN23 6NT, England.
Email: books@kingsway.co.uk

Designed and produced for the publishers by
Bookprint Creative Services, P.O. Box 827, BN21 3YJ, England.
Printed in Great Britain

Contents

Alpha

The Alpha course is a practical introduction to the Christian faith initiated by Holy Trinity, Brompton, and now being run by thousands of churches throughout the UK and overseas. It has seen extraordinary success at stimulating faith among those who are not churchgoers, and also given a new dynamism to many existing Christians.

From the Author

Is there life after Alpha?

That is the sort of question I have heard time and again. Thousands of people in scores of countries have been through the Alpha course. They are generally thrilled with it. So thrilled that some of them even do it a second time. But then what? There seems to be a lot of uncertainty.

Some of them help with setting up fresh Alpha courses.

Some of them crave for a Beta course – indeed, a number of churches have devised their own sequel to Alpha. But my impression is that a lot of people whose enthusiasm has been lit up through Alpha fail to see how the principles they learned there can be applied to church life in general and their individual lives in particular.

So what I have attempted to do in this book is very simple. It is in no sense a sequel to Alpha. It does not try to be. It is an exploration into the principles which seem to me to underlie Alpha, and an attempt to carry their implications into life after Alpha. I hope it will be of help to Christians whose discipleship has been sharpened (or even ignited) by the Alpha course. And I hope it will help clergy to see how they can deploy to the best advantage the members of their congregations who have been given new spiritual vision and vitality through the course.

That is all I am trying to do. I hope it may spark some ideas!

Michael Green
Wycliffe Hall, Oxford
Lent 1998

1

Good News to Share

The great discovery

If it was possible to gather all the hundreds of thousands
of people who have been through Alpha in one place, and
ask them the single main thing they had learned from the
experience, I think there would be little doubt as to the
answer. They would tell you that they had found a living
relationship with Jesus Christ.

Many of them will have been church members for years.
They have been attending church since they were small
children. It has been an important and meaningful part of
their lives. They would not willingly miss it. Churchgoing
seemed the right thing to do, a way of thanking God for
his goodness, a way of being spiritually refreshed to cope
with the ensuing week. But all the time they had had no
conscious relationship with Christ. One man put it very
clearly for me only the other day: 'In the past three years I
learned to give thanks to the Lord in every situation and
to praise him. Unfortunately I do not have a personal relationship with Christ, but with God in general.' Indeed,
many people who are churchgoers like this man, and
deeply serious about it, frankly do not see where Jesus fits
into the picture. God makes sense, but why bring Jesus
into it?

If that is the attitude, albeit unspoken, of many people who come to Alpha from a church background, there are many others who have rarely given God a thought until they got involved, one way or another, with Alpha. They may well come in as atheists or agnostics (which is safer!). They may be hard put to explain what they are, or why they joined the course. For some of them, Jesus may be no more than a swear word.

One of the delights of Alpha is that it brings together people from backgrounds as diverse as these. But a much greater delight is the fact that after three months in the course people from both backgrounds have a very different appreciation of Jesus, and of each other. Both have come to see that Jesus was a real historical figure, who came into this world to make God real to us and to show us what he is like. They have both come to the conclusion that, as St Paul put it, 'in him dwells all the fullness of the Godhead in bodily form'. In the words of Archbishop Michael Ramsey, 'God is Christlike, and in him is no unchristlikeness at all.' Yes, they have all come to that conclusion after studying the abundant and compelling evidence.

As if that discovery was not enough, people from both backgrounds have taken an enormous risk. They have made a great experiment. They have taken a decisive step of faith. They have come to the Jesus they now recognise as real. They have entrusted their lives to him in the best way they know how. He is like treasure hidden in a field and they have stumbled across him. Or, maybe, he is like a priceless pearl they have been looking for all their lives, and they have found him. He is the friend to whom they have been introduced. He is the honoured guest who has entered the house of their lives. He is the rock on which they have begun to build, the narrow gate through which they have squeezed to find themselves in a wonderful garden. They have discovered that Jesus is no mere man: he has brought God to our world. They have discovered that he is not dead and gone, but alive and can be met. They will tell you that they have met him. They *know* him; not just know *about* him. They do not yet know him as well as they should, nor as well as in due course they will. But he is no longer the stained-glass window Jesus, the Stranger of Galilee. They are personally linked up with him.

Now that is a life-changing discovery. Whether it comes gradually or more suddenly, whether through a friend's help or they found Jesus on their own is immaterial. They know now that he is theirs and they are his, until death, and beyond. That is the supreme discovery that thousands make during Alpha. People may have had the frame beforehand: now they have the photo to go in it. There is nothing wrong with the frame of Christianity – its churches and clergy, its services and standards. But these mean nothing without the picture. Unless we have discovered that Christianity is not primarily churchgoing, or ceremonies, or conduct, or creeds, but Christ, we have missed the most important element. Christianity *is* Christ. And most people who go through Alpha discover that, and are eternally grateful.

Very well, what are we to do with this amazing discovery after Alpha is over? The answer stares us in the face. We can help others to discover Jesus too. If we ourselves were lost in a fog beforehand, we can be sure that lots of other people are equally confused and out of touch with Jesus. The most natural thing in the world is to want to help them.

Telling your story

Sharing your experience of Christ

The easiest way to start is to tell a friend what has happened to you through your discovery of Christ. Blurt out the name of Jesus and what he has done for you. Jesus is the most wonderful name in the world. It means, literally, 'God to the rescue'. And yet the remarkable thing is that Christians are so coy about mentioning him. I sometimes listen to broadcast messages by bishops, and despite the vast numbers of people they get the chance of reaching in these opportunities, they rarely mention the name of Jesus. The church, morality, the government, the state of the nation, yes. But Jesus, no. And if that is true of our leaders, it is certainly true of most Christians. They will admit to being Christians. They will even invite a friend to church. But they decline to mention the name that is above every name – the name of Jesus. Isn't that odd? If Christianity is Christ, why are we so shy of mentioning him? And can we be surprised that people remain indifferent when we fail to let them know that Jesus is the reason for the change in ourselves?

The fact is that every one of us has a story to tell. It is as personal and individual as our fingerprints. I think it is marvellous that God should bother to make us all so special that there is nobody in the world like us. And I think it is even more wonderful that he should choose to approach each of us with respect for our individuality. Our story is unique. We will want to tell our friend about that encounter between Jesus and ourselves. We are not in the business of talking about our life or achievements. We will not major on some experience that happened to us in the past. We will want to tell them about Jesus and the difference he has made and continues to make to us.

The advantages

This is a wonderful way of helping someone to start seeking for themselves. For one thing it is intriguing. It always is to hear somebody else's experience. It is possible for any one of us: indeed, it is impossible for anyone else to tell our story with conviction! It is delightfully nonchurchy and unexpected. I mean, it is not as if the vicar called on you and told you to get right with God. You might feel that was his job, even if you found it unwelcome. But to have your partner on the golf course or your friend in the kitchen tell you the difference Jesus Christ has made to their lives – well, that is unexpected to say the least.

What is more, it is easy to do. We can all speak about ourselves and our experiences. We do it all the time – what happened at work today, what our last holiday was like, what a pain our kids were last weekend, and so forth. So why should we find it difficult to say that our greatest discovery in life has been that Jesus is alive and can be met?

Telling a friend a bit about our story of discovery has two other great advantages. In the first place it is unanswerable. Most of us are tongue-tied when talking about intimate personal matters, like sex and God. But we are particularly unwilling to get involved in any mention of our Christian faith because we fear being shot to pieces in argument. I understand. I often feel like that too. But the charm of telling your story is that you can't be shot down. It is unanswerable. Nobody can deny your experience. All they can do is to say that they have not had an experience like that, and that leaves the way open for you to smile and say, 'No reason why you shouldn't have a similar experience. Come and join the next Alpha.' So the great bogy of our fear is dealt with at a stroke if we concentrate on speaking naturally about our encounter with Christ. Nobody can deny it. Nobody can make us look foolish. And that is a great relief.

The other thing is this. Often when we have spoken quietly and honestly about our discovery we will find that a conversation opens up. Lots of people out there are longing for something to believe in, something that makes sense, something that can bring stability and joy into life. And if you, their friend, suggest that you may have begun to discover just that, well, many of them will give you a very interested hearing. They will have objections, no doubt gathered over a lifetime. They will be unclear about much of what you say to begin with. But gradually you may find that the spell of Jesus begins to grab them, and you may have the tremendous joy of enabling somebody else to discover Christ for themselves.

How can we go about it?

If you are wondering 'How can I share my story with someone else? How can I go about it when the opportunity comes?' maybe the following suggestion will be of some help. It is a good idea to have a simple outline in your mind of what you want to say so as to avoid waffling with all sorts of irrelevancies.

If you are one of those who have had a fairly sudden awakening to Christ, it would be a good idea to say a bit about your life before Christ became real to you, and in so doing to empathise as much as you can with the friend to whom you are talking. You will then want to say why and how you reached the point of Christian commitment. And naturally you will then want to give some clear examples of the difference Christ has made and continues to make in your own life. It is a story with three chapters: before Christ, meeting Christ, and life since Christ. And it's a story that needs to be kept up to date.

Very much the same holds good if you are one of the many whose Christian awakening was a more gradual thing – more like a flower slowly opening or the dawn breaking in the sky. You will want to acknowledge the Christian influences in your home and among your loved ones. You will acknowledge that God called you from your earliest days and that you are so grateful for that background. But you will want to go on to speak of the time when it all became much more personal and challenging. Your inherited faith was something you began to claim for yourself and to live by. And you will surely want to go on to speak of the changes that have taken place in your life since Christ was deliberately put in his proper place. In a nutshell, 'God called me. God challenged me. God is changing me.'

Avoiding the mistakes

Make sure that in all this you keep the focus on Jesus. What you are trying to communicate by your words and manner is the joyful result of Christ impacting your life. If you want to help your friend, be sure to avoid Christian technical terms like 'conversion', 'seeing the light', 'salvation' and so on. These will be double Dutch to your friend! Try to prune out irrelevant personal details and all exaggeration or repetition. Do not concentrate simply on the past, but show what a joy it is to have a living present relationship with Christ. That is the thing that will make an impression on your friend. Whenever you are talking on a topic like this there is the danger on the one hand of self-centredness and on the other hand of preaching. Avoid

both. Keep to the modest and joyful assertion 'I have found . . .' and you will discover that this tool of telling your story, which you have already learned in the Alpha course, can be a marvellous way of beginning to help your friends to discover Christ for themselves, whether they come from a church background or not.

If your friend is still very confused about it all, it is such a help if you explain simply and naturally how you found Jesus. Personal testimony from a trusted friend has enormous power. Just think of the woman of Samaria, recorded in the Gospel of John chapter 4. She had a very limited exposure to Jesus, but it was more than enough to change her life. She understood very little, merely that Jesus was the long-awaited deliverer and that he could make a spring of water bubble up in the arid desert of her life. But it was enough. Armed with those two discoveries she hurried to the men she knew so well back in the village,

and told them about a real Man who had made all the
difference to her. The result? In due course they came to
discover him for themselves. That could happen in your
experience too, as you tell your story humbly, humorously
and naturally to a friend who has expressed interest. You
don't need to be sitting in an Alpha course. You can do it
whenever opportunity offers – in a car, at the kitchen sink,
at work, or when waiting around to bat in a game of
cricket. One of the things for which Alpha has equipped
you is being able to speak without embarrassment and
without pious language about the greatest discovery of
your life.

Taking it further

Telling your story is likely to open up interesting conversations. Your friends may want to tell you something of their
story, and may want to know how they can begin a serious
enquiry into Christianity. There are a number of things
you might do.

An invitation to Alpha

You might invite your friend to join the next Alpha course
in your area. There is a lot to be said for that. If it has been
a real help to you, it will probably be no less valuable for
your friend. Moreover it will be led by competent people
who are capable of answering thoughtful questions about
the faith, and have some experience in helping enquirers to
discover Christ personally. What is more, it will engage
your friend in a three-month series of evenings in which
there is every reason to suppose he or she will get a
rounded exposition of the basics of the Christian faith
and will be in the company of others engaged on the same
journey. So that would be my first suggestion. Get them

into the next Alpha course. And if they won't go without you, either go with them for the first week or two to get them settled, or else go through the course with them to keep them company. You are sure to learn more yourself this way as well.

An invitation to church

Another thing you might do is to invite them to come to church with you. This is a bit more problematic, because many churches are not the best way of helping the casual enquirer. The liturgy is complicated. The ceremonial may well strike them as obscure. The fellowship may not be very warm and welcoming. The Christian assumptions behind the worship may seem alien. The opportunities for discussion and enquiry may be very few: services tend to be run from the front, with no opportunity for talk-back. Above all, the church may not be designed to make newcomers feel at home, but may be intended to keep the conservatively minded longtime churchpeople happy with what they are used to. And nowadays, with a massive gap in culture, language and assumptions between the church and the rest of society, that is a very serious disadvantage indeed. So serious that many ordinary people would no more feel comfortable going into a church than I would into a Masonic hall.

Nevertheless, it may be right for some of your friends. I can think of people who have started coming to church after an experience of loss, after a bereavement, or even after moving house. They have gradually been drawn into the worshipping community and have become Christians by osmosis. That tends to happen in the more Catholic churches, where the approach is not so much through explanation as through adoration; not so much through the word as through the sacrament. People are drawn to the mystery of the Beyond in their midst, and they gradually realise that it is through Jesus that this becomes possible.

So I would not rule out the expedient of taking a friend along to church with you. It has brought many people to real faith. But it is a risky business unless you are very confident that your church is one which is really suited to the needs of your friend. And it goes against one of the important principles of Alpha. You may recall how, in all probability, your Alpha course was not held in a church building at all. It may have been in a home, in a church hall or even in a pub. The point is that it was held on neutral ground, where visitors were not made to feel at a disadvantage compared with those who came regularly. But as a newcomer to a church service, they do feel at a disadvantage. That is something it may be wise to avoid.

A talk with the minister

What other options are there? Well, you could refer them to your vicar or pastor. This has the great advantage of putting the enquirer in touch with someone with more understanding and experience than you have at present. On the other hand, your friend may not know or necessarily trust your pastor, but they do know and trust you. So what you may gain in expertise by referring them to a more experienced person you lose in relationship. And that is a serious loss, because your friend is unlikely to be so open in sharing her thoughts and feelings with a comparative stranger as she is with you.

There are other disadvantages. The pastor in question may not have the time or the gifts required. Time will no doubt eventually be found, although it may be too late and your friend will have gone off the boil by then. But gifting is a very different matter. Your vicar may never have led an enquirer to faith in the course of his whole ministry. Particularly in the Anglican Church, people are ordained because of intellectual and pastoral rather than evangelistic gifts, and many parish priests have never seen an atheistic or agnostic adult become a committed Christian. Indeed, some of them think it should never happen! I have known college chaplains tell students who have been converted to Christ during some university mission or other that it will soon wear off and that it was merely a passing emotional experience! So it may not be such a good idea to refer your friend to the pastor. Naturally I am sketching a 'worst case' scenario. Plenty of vicars and pastors are very skilled at helping people to find a living faith, and have a passion to do it. It's a question of knowing your pastor, and being sure that he has the requisite gifts and concern to help your enquiring friend.

The loan of a book

Another thing you might do is to build up a bookshelf of well-written, highly readable books which explain the Christian faith clearly and attractively to an enquirer. Then you can say to your friend who expresses interest in Christian things, 'May I lend you this book? It is very readable, and it puts these things a lot better than I can.' Lend him or her the book, and suggest that you meet for a meal in a couple of weeks' time when you can discuss it. You will find that the book has done most of the work for you, and it may be quite easy then to help your friend towards a clear commitment to Christ. Naturally you do not want to give him some massive theological tome, but rather something that is sound biblical Christianity, attractively presented.

There are not many people who write books like that for people who are not yet persuaded. The most distinguished such author this century has been C. S. Lewis. In particular his *Mere Christianity* has helped thousands to faith. And those who do not respond to the rational arguments in a book like that are often entranced into Christian faith through the imagination and storytelling of his Narnia books. Steve Chalke has an enormous following now through his television work, and he has the ability to explain the good news of Jesus in a very readable way. His *More than Meets the Eye* is a useful book to have on that shelf of yours. So is Steve Gaukroger's *It Makes Sense*. Nicky Gumbel himself is superb at writing with depth and attractiveness for unchurched people, and any of his books such as *Questions of Life*, *Searching Issues* and *A Life Worth Living* would be helpful to almost anyone. If you have been through Alpha, you will almost certainly have read his introductory booklet to the Christian faith, *Why Jesus?* Have a few of those ready to lend, or Norman Warren's excellent booklet that has passed the test of time, *Journey into Life*.

The most powerful exposure of Western apathy about the things of God and intelligent advocacy of the Christian cause comes from Bishop Lesslie Newbigin. It must be said that his books are for the more intellectually inclined, but they are invaluable. After a brilliant academic career and a lifetime in India, he produced in his semi-retirement in Britain a series of books which are extremely helpful both for the thoughtful enquirer, and for the puzzled minister who wonders why people do not respond. *Foolishness to the Greeks*, *The Gospel in a Pluralist Society*, *Truth to Tell* and *A Proper Confidence* are all invaluable.

I too have tried to write a good deal for the person who is not persuaded of the truth of Christianity. *Why Bother with Jesus?*, *Who Is this Jesus?*, *Critical Choices*, *You Must Be Joking* and *Strange Intelligence* are readily available. I do not just hope this sort of writing helps people to faith; I know it does. I find myself travelling widely and speaking in a variety of countries, and after most meetings someone will come up to me and tell me that one of my books helped them to discover Christ. That brings me great joy. Of course it is only the good Lord himself who brings about the change in people's hearts and makes Christ real to them, but it is a privilege to be the channel he uses. Books can provide that channel, and you can make them available.

Pointing the way

But the way may be open for you to help your friend to Christ there and then. This has often happened to me. Of course nothing is as sudden as it seems. There is always a long period in a person's life that leads up to the critical issue. And there is always a long period of growth and adjustment to follow. But what if your friend says to you something like: 'I'm fascinated by what you tell me about meeting up with Jesus. As a matter of fact I have been looking in this direction for some time. I don't have problems about who Jesus was and the reality of it all, but I simply don't know how I can connect up with him'? What then? Are you going to say, 'Well, you must wait three months until the next Alpha begins'? Or, 'I must introduce you to my vicar'? Or, 'Here's a book you might like to read'? Perhaps. But it might just be right for you to take things a bit further yourself. After all, you are his friend. He has confided in you. He may not like your vicar. He may not want to wait three months for an answer. He may not be a reader. But he will talk to you.

Some basic outlines

So how can you go about it? Well, it helps to have a simple outline in your mind that you can develop appropriately for your friend. There are lots of them about. *The Four Spiritual Laws* is one. John Stott's *Becoming a Christian* is another. The New Testament had one: repent, believe and be baptised. But I am going to give you a couple of possible outlines which you might find helpful to think over and make your own.

The first such outline is very easy to remember. It is based on the first four letters of the alphabet. You suggest to your friend that if he or she wants to find a living faith in Christ these are four appropriate stepping stones. There is something to admit, something to believe, something to consider and something to do. Not original, but none the worse for that!

There is *something to admit* if you are going to get right

with God. And that is the simple fact that you have blown it. Your deeds, your words, your attitude to God, your character are all infected by the human disease that the Bible calls sin. It is the result of humanity making a unilateral declaration of independence against God, and it runs through the bloodstream of us all. There is not a man, woman or child who is free of it. And the sense of emptiness, the lack of meaning, and the confusion in our lives are all due to this fundamental problem: we are in the wrong with God. We are facing the pain of living without God in a world where the only lasting joy is to live in company with God. To put it more specifically, we have broken God's laws for human life and happiness (1 John 3:4). We have come short of the standards he expects – standards expressed in the life of Jesus (Romans 3:23). We have turned our backs on his love for us and his authority over us (John 3:18). As a result we find ourselves estranged from God (Isaiah 59:1–2; Ephesians 2:1) and in bondage to our selfishness (John 8:34; Titus 3:3; 2 Peter 2:19). Moreover, this human disease is fatal if it is not dealt with (Romans 6:23). So if we are going to get right with God we begin by recognising that we are in the wrong with God. We must be willing for a change. And don't think it will be easy to get your friend to jump this first hurdle. It won't be. You are battling against the primal sin of human pride, which finds it incredibly hard to say, 'I was wrong. I am really sorry.' But your friend will get nowhere until he makes that humbling admission.

Second, there is *something to believe* if we are going to mend relationships with the God who loves us but is affronted by the sort of people we have allowed ourselves to become. Mercifully we do not have to believe a great deal in order to become a Christian. The content of a person's faith will grow in the days and months that follow. It is interesting that the earliest Christian confession was simply: 'Jesus is Lord.' Actually, that says it all. 'Jesus' means 'God to the rescue', as we have already remarked, and 'Lord' is the name often used in the Bible for God. So what this short confession means is something like: 'God himself has come to our rescue on the cross. And he is risen and exalted as Lord of the universe, of the church and of me personally.' That is God's answer to our problem, in a nutshell. He became incarnate for us, died for us, rose to an endless life for us and calls for our allegiance.

You may need to take time to explain all this the best you know how, because it will probably be quite new to your friend. It may take time for him to grasp how brilliantly and precisely God has met our need, how wonderfully he has devised a cure for the 'human disease'. Through his death on the cross Jesus dealt with our guilt by taking personal responsibility for it (2 Corinthians

5:21; Romans 5:1; 8:1; 1 Peter 3:18). And because of the resurrection he is alive, and can be met. He can become our companion in this life and our sure guide to the life to come. After all, nobody else has risen from the dead! No wonder St Peter could not keep quiet about it: 'Praise be to the God and Father of our Lord Jesus Christ! In his great mercy he has given us new birth into a living hope through the resurrection of Jesus Christ from the dead' (1 Peter 1:3, NIV). And just as Christ's death cleans up the record of our accusing past, so his resurrection can release in our lives a power which makes for radical change. The risen and living Lord offers to come and take up residence in our lives so as to enable us to share in the power of his resurrection (Ephesians 1:19; 1 Peter 1:3–5; Philippians 4:13, 19). That is what you are encouraging your friend to believe. Not a lot, but highly significant. Not a creed, but a person: the person of the living God who came and died and rose. And it is not a fairy story, but firmly anchored in history. It is eminently worthy of belief.

Third, there is *something to consider*. And that is the cost of discipleship. It has been well said that the entrance fee to the Christian life is free (because Christ paid it), but the annual subscription is everything we have. The point is that Jesus confronts us not simply as Saviour but as Lord. And you will save your friend a lot of trouble and disillusionment later on if you make it very plain at the outset that it is no picnic but a costly thing to be a real Christian. Jesus laid it on the line very clearly in Luke 14:25–35 immediately after emphasising, in the parable of the Great Supper, that the kingdom is gloriously free to all comers. But he went on to ask if people were ready to put allegiance to him even before family ties. Were they ready to face hardship and opposition for their faith? Were they willing often to be in the minority? Elsewhere he asked if they were ready to be salt and light in society. These were some of the elements in the costly discipleship to which Jesus called people. They have not changed!

I sometimes summarise it like this. Jesus asks us to be willing to forego three s's: no *sin* held on to (1 John 3:6); no *self* promoted before him (Matthew 6:24); no *secrecy* about allegiance to him (Romans 10:9–10). Now of course that is an ideal to aim for. It does not mean that your friend will always attain it, as you very well know from your own experience. He will often sin. He will often put self before Christ. He will often be ashamed to acknowledge whose he is and whom he serves. But those three s's remain on God's Standing Orders for those who sign up in his forces. Of course the Christian life costs even more than this. But it is rather like marriage. The cost seems tremendous when you are wondering whether or not to get married, but once you are married, it seems negligible (in a good marriage!) compared with the joy of partnership with the one you love. So it is with Jesus. It costs a lot to follow him, but it costs even more to reject him.

Fourth, there is *something to do*. In a sense, of course, Jesus has done all that is necessary to bring us to God. It is a gift, not something we can ever earn. But even a gift has to be received. And so does the gift of God which is eternal life (Romans 6:23). He offers it to us freely, but we have to receive it. That makes sense, does it not? Your friend will quickly see the point.

The question is, how can he go about receiving something he cannot see and responding to someone who appears not to be around? That is where faith comes in. Faith is not trying to believe what you know is not true. It is trusting someone reliable. And who could be more reliable than God? I find it helpful at this stage to take my friend to John 3:16, probably the best-known verse in the whole Bible. It explains mankind's great need ('perishing'), God's great love (he even 'sent his Son') and it makes clear the importance of response by a decisive act of faith ('whoever believes in him'). Now maybe your friend will think that he already believes, after a fashion. So it might be helpful to turn back a page to John 1:12, so as to help him see what the Bible really means by believing: 'To all who received him, to those who believed in his name, he gave the right to become children of God' (NIV). That makes it perfectly clear that believing is no vague assent to some proposition or other, but self-commitment on good evidence. 'Believing' is 'receiving'. Your friend knows how to receive a gift. He knows how to receive a friend into his home. Very well, that is what it means to receive Jesus Christ.

There is a verse in the Bible that has helped millions of people to take that decisive step of faith for themselves. Jesus Christ, risen and ascended, is addressing a church in Asia Minor, the church at Laodicea. They think highly of themselves: they are rich, successful and have need of nothing. But Jesus looks through them with laser eyes. He sees that they are wretched, pitiable, poor, blind and naked. He offers to clothe them. He offers to give them 20/20 vision. He offers to entrust to them true riches. Indeed, he offers to come himself into their impoverished lives. 'Repent,' says Jesus. He means we need to change direction. We have been looking away from him all these years, although we may, like the Laodiceans, have been quite religious. So Jesus makes his magnificent offer: 'Here I am! I stand at the door and knock. If anyone hears my voice and opens the door, I will come in and eat with him, and he with me' (Revelation 3:20, NIV).

What eloquent imagery! Our lives, however religious we may be, are 'wretched, pitiable, poor, blind and naked' until we make room for the divine visitor, who stands at our door and knocks for admission. He has every right to enter. After all, he made the house of what we fondly call our lives. And when we had stolen it from him by our self-centredness he bought the property back at enormous cost on Calvary. But he is too much of a gentleman to force his way into the house that is, by rights, doubly his. He waits for the tenant to ask him in. And that is precisely what your friend needs to do if he is going to begin a real relationship with Christ. And you may have the inestimable privilege of helping him to take that momentous step. You may not be able to answer all his questions, but you will be clear enough on the central issue, because it is so fresh in your own experience.

I sometimes find it a help to ask my friend if he is clear enough to make a decision. If he is not, I try to see what the problem is and help him to find a way through it. If he says he is ready, I ask him if he would like to take that step of opening up on his own, or whether he would rather have me around when he does so. Usually he opts for the latter. In which case, I suggest we pray. I then pray for him or her, asking God to give them the courage to take the most important decision in their lives, and then say, 'Right, it's your turn now.' Sometimes they will say, 'What? You expect *me* to pray?' I reply that I do. They often add, 'You don't mean out loud, do you?' To which I reply, 'God can hear you just as well if you pray silently, but I can't, and I thought you wanted to have me share in all this with you? Just speak to Jesus in your own words, claim the promise he has made, and ask him to come by his unseen self, his Holy Spirit, and start living in your life. He will do just that. He has promised, and he won't break his word.' It is profoundly moving to hear a friend pour her heart out to the Lord and ask him to come and take up residence within. I know of no joy like it. And that joy can be yours. After all, you are just one grateful beggar telling another needy beggar where he can get bread.

There you have it. That is the main outline I have used over many years and I have seen hundreds of people come to share that experience of the living Christ which God has given to me. I have deliberately given you a few verses of the Bible as I have gone through it. They may be of help to you as you chat with others.

The bridge

But do you remember that I mentioned another outline just now? I would like to share it with you very briefly. It is built around the concept of a bridge. On one side is God. On the other side, human beings. There is a wide gulf in between, which is to be expected, since God is the Creator and we are the creatures, but also because God is holy and we are not. Explain to your friend how very aware people are today of this existential gap – this sense of alienation – even if they don't feel particularly guilty and are far from sure that God even exists. They know there is an emptiness within them. You can then show how, down the ages, people have run out little pontoon bridges to try to span that gap. Religion, good deeds and sincerity are the main three, though there are others. The trouble is that none of them reaches over the chasm to God. Religious observance is good, but it may well be insincere, formal or even mercenary – a sort of heavenly insurance policy. The Bible is very strong against this sort of thing: 'These people honour me with their lips, but their hearts are far from me' (Isaiah 29:13, NIV). Good deeds are obviously pleasing to the heart of God. But good deeds can never earn us a place in his home, any more than your good deeds towards me could make you a member of my family. In any case, many of our motives for these good deeds are mixed. No, that will not do. As for sincerity, of course God wants sincerity in us, but sincerity is not enough. I can be sincere and wrong. I often am. I may sincerely believe a road will take me towards London when it takes me towards Nottingham instead! None of those bridges will get us across the great divide.

And then you show your friend that God has built a bridge from his side, and it is properly anchored on both sides of the divide. The bridge, of course, is Jesus, and it reaches both sides because he is both truly God and truly man – unlike anyone else who has ever lived. He comes both to reveal to us what God is really like, and to rescue us from our alienation. That bridge is cross-shaped. It points to the tremendous cost he willingly paid in order to bring us back. You can show your friend that Jesus who came to find him is longing to take him by the hand and lead him back over the bridge to the Father's family. All he has to say in order to make a start is, 'Yes please . . . and thank you, Jesus.'

Now nobody would pretend that this is the end. It is not even, in Churchill's famous words, the beginning of the end. But it is the end of the beginning, and you have been the agent in bringing it about. What a privilege!

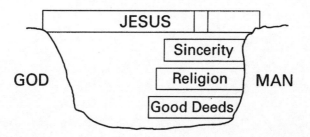

Well, these are some of the ways that you can operate after Alpha. You can take the central lesson of the whole course, an introduction to Jesus, and pass that priceless gift on to others in a variety of ways, some of which I have explored in this chapter.

And finally, a word for the pastor or vicar who has ex-Alpha people in his parish. You have a tremendous asset in these people. They have come to a living faith in Christ, and they can be encouraged and indeed trained to pass it on to others in the church community who don't quite see it yet, and also to those beyond the walls of the church. Train them. Encourage them. Give them their heads. For in them you have a potential commando force, determined to know Christ better and to make him known.

2

Proper Confidence

They were discussing it only today on the radio. What is the purpose of life – if there is one? That is a question that exercises a lot of people these days when we seem to have everything to live with but nothing much to live for. 'There remains deep in the soul (if I dare use that word) a persistent and unconscious anxiety that something is missing, some ingredient that makes life worth living.' Those were Prince Charles' words, and he has good reason to make the comment after all he has been through. But the feeling is very widespread. There is a lyric in Bruce Springsteen's 'Born in the USA' that expresses very well the meaninglessness which many people feel:

> I get up in the morning
> And I ain't got nothing to say
> I come home in the evening
> I go to bed feeling the same way
> I ain't nothing but tired,
> Man, I'm just tired and bored with myself.

Many would identify with the following words of an attractive young woman: 'I'm just a collection of mirrors, reflecting what everyone else expects of me.' To me one of the most memorable expressions of modern confusion about self-identity and meaning was provided by the distinguished columnist Bernard Levin of *The Times*:

> To put it bluntly, have I time to discover why I was born before I die? I have not managed to answer that question yet, and however many years I have before me they are certainly not as many as there are behind. There is an obvious danger in leaving it too late. . . . Why do I have to know why I was born? Because, of course, I am unable to believe it was an accident, and if it wasn't one, it must have a meaning.

Maybe you shared that confusion and lack of ultimate purpose in life before you went on an Alpha course? If not, you will certainly know many people who do. But I imagine that one of the things that Alpha has done for you is to give you a quiet confidence you never had before – a willingness to look these uncomfortable ultimate questions in the eye and have an assured answer to give.

Confidence in who you are

Who am I?

There must have been times, perhaps when you couldn't get to sleep, or stood on a cloudless night under the canopy of stars, when you wondered, 'Who am I? Where did I really come from?' There are only two basic answers to that question.

One answer sees a human being as little more than a complex of chemical entities, a grown-up bunch of genes, a load of atoms in suspension. That is the atheist answer. That is what many scientists think. In the *Sunday Telegraph*, on 7 April 1996, Peter Atkins wrote: 'The human race must realise how insignificant it is. We are just a bit of slime on a planet belonging to one sun.' That conclusion is inescapable if there is no God. For without a creator there is no meaning or purpose for life. 'Man real-

ises that he is an accident, a completely futile being, who has to play out the game without reason.' Such was the conclusion of the painter Francis Bacon, and on humanist grounds I do not see how we could dispute it.

But there is another possibility: that we are the products of a divine intelligence we call God. That is no mere whistling in the wind to keep our courage up in a chilly world. No, there is good evidence for God. It has been well said that if God did not exist we would have had to invent him. There are so many facts that point in his direction.

There is *the fact of the world*, for one thing. Nothing comes from nothing, does it? Very well, here we have a very complicated something, our universe. Had it no cause, no source outside itself? That is a fashionable view today, but it is frankly ludicrous. If you were to go to the heart of Papua New Guinea, where they had never met a white man or heard of Christianity, and tell them that on the other side of the world there are people who believe that the whole universe came into being by a series of accidents, and that it functions like a machine but, unlike any other machine, it had no designer and has no purpose, they would look at you with pity and say, 'They must be a very superstitious tribe over there.' How can our world have originated by chance when it is shot through with cause and effect? The atheist explanation of the world is very unconvincing.

Then there is *the fact of design*. Think of the focusing equipment of an eye, the radar of a bat, the built-in gyroscope of a swallow. Think of the perfect harmony of the laws of physics. Or think of the marvel of a foetus developing in the womb. As the agnostic John Stuart Mill wryly observed, 'The argument from design is irresistible. Nature does testify to its Creator.' Today physicists talk about the anthropic principle, the fact that our world seems to be precisely designed for the emergence of human life. Had its oxygen, its gravity and so forth been even marginally different, there could have been no life on this planet. It bears the marks of design. And design requires a Designer.

Next there is *the fact of personality*. The difference between a person and a thing, between a live person and a corpse, is fundamental. My personality cannot be explained merely in terms of matter. I am more than matter. But how come if there is no God? Does a river run higher than its source? Of course not. Then how do we get human personality out of raw, inorganic matter if there is no God? Can rationality and life spring from non-being and chance? No, the fact of personality is a strong pointer to the God who makes us in his image.

The *fact of values* points in the same direction. C. S. Lewis developed the point powerfully in his *Mere Christianity*. The moment you admit one course of action is better than another you are driven to accept a standard by which all moral actions are assessed. We all have our values, but they do not fit very well with the atheist's picture of a world sprung from time, chance and impersonal matter. I do not see much basis for value judgements there. But if there is a creator God, then beauty, truth, goodness, communication and life itself are all his gift and reflect his nature.

Conscience is another fact of life. That is a pointer to God if ever there was one. Your conscience does not argue. It acts like a lawgiver inside you, acquitting or condemning you. And the presence of a law suggests a Lawgiver. Conscience cannot be explained away as the pressure of society. All great moral reforms have been carried out in the name of conscience by those who faced tremendous opposition from society: think of Wilberforce ending the slave trade, or Martin Luther King championing the cause of black people. Conscience is a clear pointer to a God who is no blind force, no abstruse designer, but a personal God, so concerned about right and wrong that he has put a moral indicator into each one of his creatures.

Then there is *the fact of religion*. All over the world and all through history there have been atheistic individuals, but there has never been an atheistic nation or tribe, and modern attempts to get rid of God, as in communist states, have boomeranged into religious revivals. You can see it in Russia and China. Worship is instinctive in human beings, and if we do not worship God we worship idols. The major contemporary ones in the West are money, sex and power. But these are all God-substitutes. All our other instincts – for food, sex, sleep and so forth – have the appropriate reality to satisfy them. Is our instinct to worship the only exception? Should we not see it as a powerful pointer to the God who desires our company?

But *much the most powerful pointer to God's reality is Jesus Christ*. His contemporaries, strict Jewish monotheists though they were, came to the unshakable conclusion that he was the visible expression of the invisible God. His character, his teaching, his influence, his claims, his death, his resurrection all support that conviction. The God to whom there are so many pointers has come to find us!

That is how you see it now, do you not? The Alpha course has helped you out of the fog; you are emerging under clear blue skies. You know who you are. Behind your parents and centuries of forebears is the personal, living God. The evidence is reliable. You have committed yourself, and you are finding it true. I love the first chapter of Ephesians, where the apostle Paul, although imprisoned in a horrible gaol, is bubbling with joy in the God who 'chose us in [Christ] before the foundation of the world' (v. 4). What a confidence that gives. Before I even existed I was the object of his love. He 'destined us in love to be his sons through Jesus Christ' (v. 5). I know who I am. Frail, sinful, ageing, I can stand high. I am adopted into the family of the King of kings. And he has a purpose for our lives. We are meant to live 'to the praise of his glory'. That is something to sing about. That is a rock-solid foundation on which to build a life. I know where I come from: he chose me before the foundation of the world. I know what my business is: to reflect his glory.

What am I worth?

But if I know who I am, there is another great uncertainty. What am I worth? Here again we must choose between two alternatives. The atheist answer is stark and sombre. I may have value as a mate, as a producer, but ultimately I have none. I am just another bit of jetsam on the cosmic beach. After all, my wife may leave me, my parents may disinherit me, my kids may scorn me. I may get made redundant at the drop of a hat in today's economic climate. I can be earning £30,000 on Friday and by Saturday I can be on the dole. No, I am not worth much on the atheist account.

But there is another possibility. What if this living God values me greatly? What if he thinks me worth coming to find, although I am so far from him? What if he thinks me worth the ultimate sacrifice – of his life to redeem mine? What then? In the same first chapter of Ephesians Paul revels in that truth: 'In [Christ] we have redemption through his blood, the forgiveness of our sins, in accordance with the riches of God's grace which he lavished upon us' (vv. 7–8, NIV). That makes Paul dance for joy in his cell. At the cross I see God smiling through his tears and saying to Paul – and to me – 'See how much you are worth. You are infinitely valuable to me. I made you in my image. I came to find you when you ran away. I went to that terrible cross in order to rescue you. I offer you pardon for the past, and liberation from that dark side of your life which at times you curse yourself for and which I cannot abide. I gave everything to set you free and win you back That's how much I think you are worth.' And where is the solid evidence? The cross of Jesus.

How can I cope?

Often that is the despairing cry of the mother with four children under seven, of the teenager torn between childhood and adulthood, the overworked executive, or the lonely unemployed person. How can I cope?

Once again, there are only two answers. Once again, we have to choose. One answer says, 'Well, it's just too bad. You'll have to put up with it. You're on your own. Do your best. Self-effort – that's all there is.'

The other says, 'That is a lie. The Lord who made you, who died for you, is alive and well. Unlike any other great teacher in the world he is willing and able to come and live inside you by his unseen Holy Spirit. And that Holy Spirit can grow something of the moral power, the joy, the unselfishness of Jesus in the soil of your life.' Paul and his converts at Ephesus had discovered the truth of that: '[You] who have heard the word of truth, the gospel of your salvation, and have believed in him, were sealed with the promised Holy Spirit, which is the guarantee of our inheritance until we acquire possession of it' (Ephesians 1:13–14). The apostle uses two fascinating pictures of the Holy Spirit in that sentence. One word speaks of the stamp of God's personal possession. The Spirit is his mark that we belong. The other speaks of a first instalment; indeed in modern Greek the word is used for an engagement ring! The Holy Spirit is God's engagement ring, his pledge of heaven given to us while we are still on earth. The Holy Spirit is the only part of the future that we can enjoy now. And as for those besetting habits that pull you down, Paul is confident that the indwelling Holy Spirit offers us the very same power which raised Christ from the tomb! He prays that they may know 'the immeasurable greatness of his power . . . which he accomplished in Christ when he raised him from the dead' (Ephesians 1:19–20). Yes, the Holy Spirit is solid evidence that we are not left to struggle on our own, and I have no doubt that since your time in Alpha, if not before, you have tasted the reality of his presence and his life-changing power.

Where am I headed?

That is another cry of today's world which is so short of purpose, meaning, or confidence in the future. And here again there are only two choices we can opt for.

One is the atheist view. It is eloquently expressed by J. H. Blackman, the leading British humanist: 'On humanist assumptions life leads to nothing, and any claim to the contrary is a cruel deceit.'

'What is our life?' asked Jean-Paul Sartre. 'Nothing but a crumpled piece of paper in the rain.'

Or, as Bertrand Russell bluntly put it, 'When I die I rot.' That is all there is to it. The body rots. The lights go out.

The other answer is breathtaking in its bold claim. Our destiny is to know God and enjoy him for ever. Or, as the Bible puts it, 'to depart and be with Christ, for that is far better' (Philippians 1:23). Better because we shall be gathered into God's home where ' ". . . he will wipe away every tear from their eyes, and death shall be no more, neither shall there be mourning nor crying nor pain any more, for the former things have passed away." And he who sits upon the throne said, "Behold, I make all things new"' (Revelation 21:4–5).

We have to choose between those two views of death and its sequel. Paul has no doubt about it, and in that same first chapter to the Ephesians he revels in anticipation in the glory of God's inheritance for his people (Ephesians 1:14). But what grounds has he for such confidence? What grounds have we?

The answer lies in the resurrection of Jesus Christ. As you will have studied in the Alpha course there is overwhelming evidence that Jesus, alone of the great teachers of the world, broke the death barrier and rose triumphant from the grave. What is more, you know him. You know something of the power of his resurrection in your own life. That resurrection from the grave is the most solid assurance that Christian hope for the future is not a pipe dream. It is the pointer in the midst of history to the glorious climax to which all things are moving. No wonder Paul declares: 'Blessed be the God and Father of our Lord Jesus Christ, who has blessed us in Christ with every spiritual blessing in the heavenly places' (Ephesians 1:3).

All this brings great confidence. You know who you are, adopted sons and daughters of the living God, chosen by him before your birth. You know how valuable you are in the sight of the one who came and died for you. You know you have his mighty Spirit within you, and his home awaits you at the end of the road. No wonder you can have a deep confidence whatever hardships you, like the apostle Paul, have to go through. You have faced up to the most fundamental questions of our human existence. You have looked into the options and made your choice. And that choice has excellent evidence to support it.

Confidence in being a Christian

This confidence in who we are spills over into a deep assurance about our position in Christ. And this is important, particularly in these days when people are very suspicious of assurance of any kind. Of course the cockiness and brashness that you sometimes find in Christians (as in others) is most unattractive, and the Bible gives no grounds for it. We have not arrived. We are on a journey, and it will not end until we die. Spiritual arrogance is particularly unpleasant and it ought never to be seen in Christians. After all, we owe our position as Christians to Christ alone. There is nothing to be big-headed about. What is more, our lives are still very much a battlefield. If St Paul found that (see Romans 7) we should not be surprised if we have many a struggle to face. Arrogance and over-confidence are out.

But most modern Christians, at least in the mainline

churches, are not in danger of that particular failing. By far the biggest problem is the fact that so many in our churches would be hard put to tell you whether they are Christians at all. There is massive confusion on this point. People are very ignorant of what the New Testament teaches us about it. As a result they may say, 'Well, I'm an Anglican, but I have no idea if I am a Christian.' I have had that said to me more than once! Or they will say, 'I'm not sure. I sometimes feel I am and sometimes not.' Or again, 'I try hard to be a Christian, but I really don't know.'

Some of the people who talk like this probably are still lost in the fog. They have never discovered the Jesus who is at the heart of Christianity. They give a passing thought to the manger at Christmas, the cross on Good Friday, the tomb on Easter Day, but they do not know the occupant. Perhaps the same was true of you before you went through Alpha? At all events, you will agree with me that large numbers of churchpeople have no idea whether or not they are actually Christians, because there is so much confusion about what a Christian is.

But *you* know very well that a Christian is someone who has a living relationship with Christ. That is what the word means, and without that we are not Christians, however many good turns we do to people, however sincere we are, however often we go to church or say the creed. 'Any one who does not have the Spirit of Christ does not belong to him,' says the apostle (Romans 8:9).

And one of the really useful things you can do, if you are confident of where you stand with the Lord and why, is to help others to that same proper assurance. You see, we are meant to know we belong in the family. I know I am a citizen of the UK. I do not think it, hope that it is so, or imagine that some days I am and some days I am not. I may not be a very admirable citizen, but I belong. Or think of marriage. If you ask me whether or not I am married, I can give you a clear answer. I do not hesitate, look embarrassed, or say that sometimes I feel married and sometimes I don't. No, I look you in the face and say, 'Yes indeed. I am married to Rosemary, and we have just celebrated our fortieth anniversary. I have often failed as a husband, I do not love her as I should. I do not always understand her. But we belong together. I am married.' Well, it is like that with Christ. Every Christian is meant to know that he or she belongs. It is our birthright.

Often people are frightened to claim the name of Christian in case they give the impression that they are claiming to be better than others. That is no part of Christian assurance. Saying that I am a Christian simply means that I am committed to Christ and he is committed to me. I am as sure about it as I am of my citizenship or my marriage.

Now you went into all this in the Alpha course. You saw how the whole Trinity is committed to assuring us that we belong. Do you recall the outline Nicky Gumbell used? He spoke of the word of God, the work of Jesus and the witness of the Spirit as a triple ground for confidence. Let's go over that ground afresh for a moment.

We have *the word of the Father*. 'This is the testimony, that God gave us eternal life, and this life is in his Son. He who has the Son has life; he who has not the Son of God has not life.' Those words of John (1 John 5:11–12) are reinforced by a very strong statement: 'He who does not believe God has made him a liar.' Obviously God does not lie. He can be trusted. If he tells us that in receiving his Son we have received eternal life, there is no more to be said. We praise him, and go in confidence about our daily lives.

Second, you will recall that we have *the work of God the Son* to rely on. On the cross he paid all our debts to a holy

God. There was nothing improper about it; he was man, representing us all on that terrible cross. And there was nothing immoral about it, as if the Father was punishing the Son for our sins. No, we read that 'God was in Christ reconciling the world to himself'. The job was done, the bill paid, and it never has to be paid again. 'Christ also died for sins once for all, the righteous for the unrighteous, that he might bring us to God' (1 Peter 3:18). We may sometimes feel really bad about something we have done, and the devil will try to persuade us that we can't possibly be Christians. The way to tackle it, as I am sure you have already found, is to tell the old enemy to get lost. 'Yes, I know it was a terrible thing to do. But Christ took personal responsibility for it on the cross.' The letter to the Hebrews reminds us: 'Christ has offered for all time a single sacrifice for sins,' therefore 'if we confess our sins, he is faithful and just, and will forgive our sins and cleanse us from all unrighteousness' (1 John 1:9).

The third member of the Trinity also has a hand in our assurance. Do you recall Nicky's teaching about *the witness of the Holy Spirit* to the fact that we really are in the family? St John is very clear about it: 'We know that he abides in us, by the Spirit which he has given us' (1 John 3:24). That first letter of John is an absolute goldmine for seeing the various ways in which the Spirit seeks to assure us we belong.

There is *a new sense of pardon* – a wonderful sense that we are clean: 'If anybody does sin, we have one who speaks to the Father in our defence – Jesus Christ, the Righteous One. He is the atoning sacrifice for our sins' (1 John 2:1–2, NIV).

There is *a new desire to please God*. Previously I did not much care whether I pleased him or not. Now I begin to care very much. I do not want to hurt the one I have begun to love. 'This is how we know we are in him: Whoever claims to live in him must walk as Jesus did' (1 John 2:5–6, NIV).

There is *a new attitude to other people*. 'Anyone who does not do what is right is not a child of God; nor is anyone who does not love his brother.' And 'if anyone has material possessions and sees his brother in need but has no pity on him, how can the love of God be in him?' (1 John 3:10, 17, NIV).

There is *a new appreciation of Christian fellowship*. 'We know that we have passed from death to life, because we love our brothers' (1 John 3:14, NIV). John is speaking about brother Christians. They may have seemed a rather strange lot previously, but once you join the family you find yourself glad to be with them.

There is *a new power over temptation*. 'No-one who lives in him keeps on sinning,' says John. How is this generalisation possible? Because 'the one who is in you is greater than the one who is in the world' (1 John 3:6; 4:4, NIV).

There is *a new joy and confidence*. Not that Christians do not have to go through pain and sadness. They do. But there is an underlying joy which nobody can take from us. It comes from fellowship with the Lord and his people. Hence John is able to say, 'We write this to make our joy complete' (1 John 1:4, NIV).

There is *a new experience of answered prayer*. Prayer is no longer talking to yourself, no longer a mere ritual. Christ has broken through the sound barrier of sin and alienation, and prayer begins to become companionship with God. We share things with him, and begin to find answers coming. 'This is the confidence we have in approaching God: that if we ask anything according to his will, he hears us. And if we know that he hears us – what-

ever we ask – we know that we have what we asked of him'
(1 John 5:14–15, NIV). We do not always get what we want,
needless to say, but we do have the assurance of being
heard.

And so John sums it up: 'I write this to you who believe
in the name of the Son of God, that you may know that
you have eternal life' (1 John 5:13). Not *hope* that one day
you may get it, but *know* that you have it now, because 'he
who has the Son has life; he who does not have the Son of
God does not have life'.

None of that is news to you. It formed an important
part of the Alpha course. But it is certainly news to hundreds and thousands of churchpeople. Would it not be
marvellous if you could see your way to helping some of
them into an assured relationship with Christ? Many of
them may well be in touch with him, but they do not know
it. Nobody has shown them that this is something believers can be confident about. As a result they remain worthy
churchpeople but quite unable to help others to the faith.
You can't build the house of Christian service on wobbly
foundations. First, you have to know you belong!

What a joy and privilege it is for you to pour concrete
into those foundations so that they become firm and solid,
and your friends can know where they stand in Christ and
can reach out confidently to other people with the good
news of Christian assurance.

Confidence in getting involved

In any office or workplace you will find Christians who are
indistinguishable from the unbelievers all around them.
They keep their heads down. Why? Because they lack the
confidence we have been thinking about. In any church
you will find the same: lovely people who turn out week

after week, but they have no confidence that they belong to Christ, and no good news to pass on to anyone else during the week. Did you know that there are far more people in church on any Sunday than watch and play football on a Saturday? Yet our impact is far less. Why? Because the confidence, the commitment, the enthusiasm of the football fan is lacking in so many Christians. We do not emulate the United fans driving up the motorway with a scarf hanging out of the window! We do not, so to speak, wear the strip, or talk about last night's game. We are a silent army, a sleeping army, a downtrodden army, a forgotten army. And so we get marginalised and swept aside in the places where decisions are made. Christians do not count for a lot. Homosexuals do. Muslims do. But not Christians. We are far too confused, unsure of where we stand. And so we are silent. Folk hardly ever hear a squeak out of us.

What a pity. Christianity would never have taken off in the first century if the early Christians were like that. Those men and women were flesh and blood just like us. What they did can, in principle, be done today. Indeed, in many parts of South-East Asia and Africa it *is* being done today. But our lack of confidence in the West is a terrible handicap. And it is not necessary, as I hope you have seen as you have worked through this chapter. We have nothing to apologise for in our Christian allegiance. It is the largest faith the world has ever seen. It is the most all-embracing. It has stood the test of time. It has been embraced by millions of the most intelligent, the most courageous, the most artistic, and the most self-sacrificial people who have ever lived. What have we got to be embarrassed about? Surely we are not embarrassed about Jesus, the most exciting person the world has ever seen? Very well then, let it all hang out, as they say! You have had the privilege of going through Alpha and understanding our proper Christian confidence. So do not be shy to mention Jesus Christ in the pub when opportunity offers – and it will. Do not be ashamed to let people know that you go to worship regularly. Do not shrink from following Christ's guidelines in your business, personal and professional life. What is needed is Christians who are not wimps!

And finally, think of your local church. More of this in a later chapter, but it is sure to be short of committed workers. Only a tiny proportion of those who worship on a Sunday give any practical service in and through the church during the week. Why not give careful thought to what you would like to do as a member of the church? Think about what you are equipped to do, maybe even called to do, and go along to the vicar and tell him. Get stuck in. Every Christian is called to be a worker for Christ. If I were to ask you, 'What is your ministry for the Lord in your local church?' I wonder if you could tell me? You should be able to! For the good Lord wants to give everyone a job to do. Alas, many of his followers are too unsure as well as too spiritually deaf to hear him whisper what it is. Don't let that be the case with you!

3

The Journey

The journey of discovery

One of the vital lessons of the Alpha course is that Christianity is a journey. It is a journey into faith and a journey in faith. When I began active ministry some forty years ago, many people had speedy or even sudden conversions. It may have been conversions within the framework of Christianity and church attendance. Or it may have been people quite outside the Christian faith, who had gathered to hear a particular speaker on a special occasion. It may even have been someone you bumped into on the train. I think that in those heady days of the 1960s people were hungry for change. The whole of our society was changing at a tremendous pace, and people were ready to go off on a hippy trip to India, join a commune in the counter-culture, or make a clear-cut decision to follow Christ.

I remember speaking at an amazing, packed, hippy-type church in Vancouver back in those days. I must have preached for an hour and then they shouted out for more (that had never happened before – or since!). They were highly intelligent young people who had dropped out. The service went on for ages. I recall a woman singing in tongues and then singing an interpretation. It was unspeakably beautiful. It was there that I first heard a prophetic utterance. I recall some remarkable and instantaneous healings. I was overwhelmed. And I stood at the door as they went out, and asked lots of them how long they had been Christians. The answer varied between about a year and a day. Here was a whole church full of people who had experienced a crisis conversion.

It still happens. Only recently I was involved in an outreach in Sarawak, Malaysia, when we saw hundreds make a commitment to Christ in a decisive way, and know from that day onwards that they were Christians. Billy Graham still finds enormous response to his crusades in different parts of the world. But on the whole, and especially in the Western world, we are seeing people come to faith gradually rather more often than suddenly. I think there are a number of reasons for this.

For one thing people are much further away from Christianity than they used to be thirty years ago. They learn nothing about it in home, school or workplace. The Bible is the world's bestseller, but it lies unread. Most people do not go to church. How then can they be expected to know enough about Christianity to commit

themselves the first time they hear the gospel? Research has shown that on the whole they do not. Most adult conversions these days come gradually. To be sure, there will still be that time when they face up to Christ and decide to follow him. But they take much longer to get there. My heart sinks when I go to a church and am asked to preach evangelistically, and they tell me proudly that they have trained thirty counsellors who will be waiting for people to come forward and commit themselves to Christ at the end of the address. That is not where it is at these days! I would much rather they had trained thirty people to run Alpha courses, so that those who had been intrigued or struck by the service could be fed into a warm exploratory group that would give them three months to think it carefully through and start the journey with Christ at their own pace. But alas, many churches have not thought of that. They are trying to be third-class imitators of Billy Graham, quite unaware that the habit of calling people to the front for instant commitment only began in the last century! And when the wretched preacher does not deliver thirty customers into their hands they shake their heads and conclude that his message was not anointed!

What is more, people are most unwilling to take things on anyone else's say-so these days. Why then should we expect them to respond to Christ just because some preacher commends him? Is it not much better for them to take their time and join a course where rather than five minutes of highly programmed (but often very incompetent) 'counselling' after the address, they undertake fifteen weeks of exploration? You know how they say 'A dog is not just for Christmas'? Well, Christianity is not just for a sudden decision, but for a lifetime of discipleship. It calls for careful reflection.

There is another reason why so many people prefer this gradual approach. The discussion element in Alpha is very attractive. It shows that Christians are not afraid to face tough questions, and also that they do not mind admitting they do not have all the answers. This relaxed, open-textured approach shows that our mind is meant to be engaged, not just our feelings and our will. And it gives people a chance to get rid of their hang-ups and misunderstandings as well as raising their honest doubts and questions in a warm group where the members are encouraged to think and question for themselves. It is not surprising to learn, therefore, that the early church had a lengthy induction period, a catechumenate, when those seeking Christ worked through a lot of issues in their lives for many months before taking a step which was going to involve the whole of their future.

So for many these days becoming a Christian is a process, not a crisis. There often is a crisis, but it will come not when the preacher calls for people to come forward, but when the customer is ready to respond. It is crisis within a process, if you like, and it leads to an ongoing process – lifelong discipleship.

The accompanied journey

The idea of journey or pilgrimage is as old as time. At its most basic, it is the journey we all travel between birth and death. What Christians have called conversion occurs when we allow Jesus to come and accompany us on that journey. It is not, strictly speaking, a new journey; the landscape, the companions, the work may be just the same as they were before. But the exciting thing, what makes it seem altogether new, is the fact that it is an accompanied journey from then on. Jesus Christ joins us when we invite him (indeed, as we look back on it all we will probably realise that he had crept up on us even before we invited him!) and he undertakes never to leave us or forsake us. He gives us his word that he will never let us down or give us up.

So all Christians have an accompanied journey in this sense of the word. But in an Alpha course you get additional company. There are a number of others feeling their way towards faith in Christ, or setting out on the journey. And there is a leadership team there to keep us company, to teach and encourage, and simply be around. That is an enormous help. It is like having a party in a house instead of rattling around in it on your own. We need to be accompanied. And that is one of the reasons why Alpha is so fruitful. This basic human need for company is recognised and acted upon.

Apply that now to your present situation. You may well have been asked to help run the next Alpha course in your church or area, so you will be accompanying others who are following your own search. You may be a bit ahead of them, but you can readily empathise with their doubts and unbeliefs because you were in much the same situation not long ago. And that is such a help to them. What is more, it gives you a real sense of being useful to the Lord.

But what if there is no Alpha course for you to help run? Surely the same principle applies. People need company on the journey. They need to see it working out in another human life. So when you are talking things over with your friend, as we were thinking of earlier, it is not so much your shrewd arguments or your challenge which will be the most help. It is simply your being around. You are a Christian who is putting himself out for his friend, and believe it or not, that friend will discern Christ in you.

Not only in the words expressed,
Not merely in the deeds confessed,
But in the most unconscious way
Is Christ expressed.

Is it a calm and peaceful smile?
A holy light upon the brow?
Oh no! I felt His presence
When you laughed just now.

For me 'twas not the truth you taught,
To you so clear, to me so dim.
But when you came to me, you brought
A sense of Him.
(*Anon.*)

I think back to the days when I entrusted my life to Christ, sitting on a bench in the school cricket pavilion, among the bats and pads and boots. It was Richard Gorrie, the head boy in the school, who had been God's channel to reach me, and he did it so graciously and clearly. But did he leave me to get on with it after that? Not a bit of it. Quite apart from putting me in touch with just the right sort of Christian companionship for my age, he made a point of spending time with me once a fortnight. I would raise all my objections and difficulties, and he would handle them to my satisfaction. Then we would read a bit of the Bible together and see what we could draw from it before finally praying together. That early care meant such a lot to me. My journey was well accompanied.

So even if there is no course for enquirers (be it Alpha or some other) which can use your help, there is that friend, is there not? The one you have been telling your story to? The one you have told about the difference Jesus has made, and perhaps brought to the point where he is seriously looking for Jesus himself? Your company is going to be of priceless value to him. Not only as he struggles towards Christ, but as he grows in Christian discipleship. We are not meant to be Christians on our own. We are born into a family where there are always brothers and sisters. Look around for someone whom you can help in this way.

And never forget that the need for this sort of companionship goes on all our lives. I belong to a small group that meets regularly to eat a meal together and pray about the programmes and the personal needs that each of us has. We all make it a priority because we gain enormous strength from it. Each one of us needs company along the way in the Christian pilgrimage. You should never be a solitary Christian – unless you get imprisoned in solitary confinement!

The journey within

People these days are very worried about the prevalence and growth of the drug culture. It starts younger and younger. I remember leading a mission in a country town in British Columbia, where I asked the leaders beforehand what were the main problems of the town. Their answer stunned me: 'Drugs and drunkenness among the under tens.' That was a few years ago. And now it is everywhere.

Why do people go for these self-destructive drugs? It is partly for kicks and partly because everyone is doing it. But most of all, I think, it is because life at the end of the twentieth century is so nasty and painful for so many people that there is no hope out there; only in here. The outlook is bleak, so they take refuge in the trip within.

The Christian often faces a bleak outlook too, and he is also driven to the journey within. But it is not in order to gain an artificial high which leads to bondage and disenchantment afterwards. It is in order to share every circumstance with the Christ who shares the journey with us, by his Spirit living in our hearts. 'You have died, and your life is hid with Christ in God,' says the apostle Paul (Colossians 3:1). Nobody in all the world can separate you from him. The way to grow in stature as a Christian is to take your every circumstance to God in prayer. Paul was thinking of something like that when he wrote: 'Do not get drunk with wine, for that is debauchery; but be filled with the Spirit' (Ephesians 5:18). You get a hangover from the trip within which is escapism and which looks to addictive substances for relief, but there is no hangover from communing in your heart with the Holy Spirit of God, who will fill you and strengthen you. We never get beyond the need to tread this secret inner journey where we cast all our cares upon the one who cares for us (1 Peter 5:7).

The journey people notice

Not only are we accompanied on our journey through life, we are observed. And many of those who watch us are cynical, sceptical, and yet often wistful. They know we are Christians, and they are determined to watch to see if this Christianity makes any difference. Does the trip within show?

A friend told me a marvellous story about Mother Teresa. He had heard it from a friend of his who had been visiting the Sisters in Calcutta. This man noticed how, at the Eucharist every morning, Mother Teresa came up last, and when she received the sacrament her head tilted on one side, and her face was suffused with joy as she communed with her Lord. One day she took my friend into the ward which held the most serious cases, and one of them was dying. She cradled his head on her lap as he died, and once again her face shone radiantly and her head tilted on one side. The inner life with Christ shone out, and others could see it.

That shining life, fired by deep inner communion with Christ, was what lit up the earliest Christians. You see it on every page of the Acts of the Apostles. But there was a writer at the end of the first century or the beginning of the second, who put it in a truly memorable way. You will find this passage in the *Epistle to Diognetus*.

The distinction between Christians and other men does not lie in country or language or customs. . . . They follow local customs in clothing, food, and in the rest of life, and yet they exhibit the wonderfully paradoxical nature of their own citizenship. They live in their own countries, but as if they were resident aliens. They share all things as citizens, and yet endure all things as if they were an underclass. Every foreign country is their homeland, and every homeland a foreign country. They marry like everyone else, and have children: but they do not abort their young. They keep a common table, but not a common bed. They live in the world, but not in a worldly way. They enjoy a full life on earth, but their citizenship is in heaven. They obey the appointed laws, but they surpass the laws in their own lifestyle. They love everyone, and are universally derided. They are unknown, and roundly criticized. They are put to death, and gain life. They are poor but make many rich. They lack all things, and yet have all things in abundance. They are dishonoured, and are glorified in their dishonour. They are abused, and they call down blessings in return. When they do good they are beaten up as ne'er-do-wells: when they are beaten up they rejoice as men who are given a new life. In short, what the soul is in the body, that the Christians are in the world. The soul lives in the body but is not confined by the body, and the Christians live in the world but are not confined by the world. . . . God has appointed them to this great calling, and it would be wrong for them to decline it.

It would be wrong for us to decline it too. The journey within must show to those who are observing our visible journey through this life. God calls us to let the light shine out.

The ups and downs in the journey

The Christian pilgrimage is not an easy one. The going is often rough. There are long hard hills, sheer precipices and deep pits as well as gentle meadows and gurgling streams. And we are called to walk with Christ in good times and bad, just as he walked with his heavenly Father whether he was in the sunshine by the Lake or staggering under the cross on his way to execution.

One of the hardest lessons to learn on this journey is that following Jesus Christ does not exempt you from any of the disasters along the route. It simply gives you the blessing of his company as you go through them. He does not deliver you *from* the hard times, but he does deliver you *in* them.

I had a letter the other day from one of the most gracious missionaries I have ever known. At the end of a long career in Africa, and then back in his native New Zealand where he had become a distinguished theological college principal, he contracted cancer, and is on the way to death. There is no touch of self-pity in his letter. He just longs to serve Christ as far as he is able with his limited strength and abilities.

I think too of a great friend, Archbishop Janani Luwum of Uganda. He had to face the wrath of the bloodthirsty tyrant Idi Amin. For he had gone, as the leading representative of the Christian church in the country, and respectfully told the President that what he was doing in all the senseless slaughter that made the Nile red with blood, was wrong in the sight of God. He knew that he would suffer for that courageous act of denunciation. In fact, Amin had him shot through the mouth and his body concealed. It provoked an international outcry. But what is not so widely known is that Janani was tortured before his death, and in the torture chamber he met another Christian who eventually survived. He knelt with this man and together they prayed for the President who was torturing them. You can't do that sort of thing unless you have learned to walk with Christ in the tough times as well as in the good.

But in a curious way the easier times are often the most difficult in which to maintain a bright Christian witness. We get fat and lazy when all goes swimmingly and people speak kindly of us. We lower our guard. It is not easy to keep looking to Jesus then. We assume that we don't need to. But it is vital. I am often humbled by the amazement of

African Christians when they come to England and see how poverty-stricken our spirituality is. They see how we have made pleasure and ease and wealth our gods. They notice how we have ceased to be warriors of the cross and have become soft.

Anyone who knew George Thomas, Lord Tonypandy, will bear testimony to the radiance of his Christian life, in good times and in bad. As a lad doing local preaching in the Welsh valleys, he had struggled to know whether to be ordained or to go into politics. He became sure that the latter was the plan God had for him. And how marvellously he let his Christian life shine in the rough and tumble of being Speaker in the House of Commons. I recall his patience when he was smitten with the cancer which reduced his famous voice to a whisper. I remember too his unaffected joy at the success of others, and the way he threw himself into the enjoyment of ordinary people, never being embarrassed to speak of his Lord, but never thrusting his faith down anyone else's throat.

We must never imagine that Christianity is a sort of insurance policy against the ills of life. We shall not have an easier time than those who have no love for Christ. After all, we follow a crucified Saviour. And if Christians did have it easier than anyone else, then endless people would crowd into the Christian church for all the wrong reasons. No, the gospel does not affect our circumstances, but it makes all the difference to the way we cope in those circumstances. That is what counts.

The last journey

We all have to die, and the approach of death removes the illusions and the play acting which people often entertain in the earlier part of their lives. As we approach death, we show what we are really like. Attitudes vary enormously. Some try never to give death a thought. They have lots of irons in the fire, but what is the good of irons in the fire if the fire is going out? Others, like Thomas Hobbes, resign themselves to agnosticism: 'When I die the worms will devour my body, and I will commit myself to the great Perhaps.' Some get very angry. 'Do not go gentle into that dark night,' counselled Dylan Thomas. 'Old age should burn and rage at close of day. Rage, rage against the dying of the light.' And some face it with dread. They fear either that death is the end or that it is not. They share, perhaps, in Shakespeare's 'dread of something after death, the undiscovered country from whose bourn no traveller returns'.

The death of Princess Diana brought the subject abruptly before the world's eyes. More than two billion people mourned her in an unparalleled exhibition of grief. And nobody is entirely sure why. Perhaps it was partly because death, especially in one so young and caring, so beautiful and famous, is the ultimate obscenity in a pleasure-loving age when we think that happiness is our right. Or partly because we identify with much of Princess Diana's vulnerability and insecurity. Like her we look for love, often in vain. Like her we are confused about who we really are and what our role in life is meant to be. In a post-Christian age people no longer have any sure anchor of hope.

But we do. Our hope is founded on the resurrection of Jesus Christ from the dead. As Jack Clemo wrote in *The Invading Gospel*, 'the whole philosophy of Christian optimism is founded on the literal resurrection of Jesus Christ; the fact that his triumph was part of his earthly and corporeal existence. Truth did not for ever stay on the scaffold. Truth came down from the scaffold, walked out of the tomb, and ate boiled fish.' That conviction runs through

every Alpha course. Jesus is alive, and you and I have met
with him. But a great many of our contemporaries have
not. So it is well worth making sure we are clear about the
basis for Christian confidence in the resurrection. We have
five independent accounts of the resurrection – one at the
end of each of the four Gospels and one in 1 Corinthians
15. The outlines of the case are as follows.

The resurrection: compelling evidence

In the first place we can be sure Jesus really was dead. He
was publicly executed before large crowds. He was certi-
fied as dead both by the centurion in charge of the execution and the governor, Pontius Pilate, who had the matter
investigated. He had a spear pushed through his heart, just
to make sure. Jesus was very dead that first Good Friday
afternoon. The point would hardly be worth making were
it not that some people, desperately trying to evade the
evidence for the resurrection, argue that Jesus was not
really dead, and he revived in the cool of the tomb!

Second, the tomb was found empty. All the accounts
agree. Jesus' enemies had been working for years to see
him dead and buried, and now they had succeeded. So
they made very sure, with a guard on the tomb and an
enormous boulder over it. But on Easter morning that
tomb was empty. We can be sure his enemies did not move
the body. They were only too glad he was out of the way.
Could his friends have removed it? No, for three reasons.
They could not have got at it with the sealed tomb and the
guard in place. Second, they had scattered to their homes
and were utterly disheartened. The last thing on their
minds was a resurrection. What is more, in a short time
they would turn the ancient world upside-down with their
gospel of Christ's resurrection. For its truth they were
content to be stoned, imprisoned and executed. Would

they have done that for a fraud? If neither friend nor foe removed the body, we are left with the universal explanation of the early Christians: God raised him from the dead.

Third, Jesus appeared after his death to many witnesses. The New Testament never places undue weight on an empty tomb. It is much more interested in the living Jesus who overcame the legitimate doubts of his followers by appearing to them time and again – in a garden, on a walk, in an upstairs room, at a lakeside. Each of the Gospels tells us about such appearances, which lasted only forty days and then ended as abruptly as they had begun. These resurrection appearances have never been satisfactorily explained away. They happened. And they demonstrate that Jesus conquered death.

Fourth, the Christian church owes its origin to the resurrection. We can trace its history back to the first Easter. Belief in the resurrection was the main thing that distinguished Christians from other Jews. That belief brought the church into being and swept through the Roman Empire. That belief lights up the hearts of a third of the human race two millennia later. It simply will not go away. It grows and spreads into every nation under the sun. If it were not true it would have faded long ago.

Fifth, many millions of people then and now have encountered the risen Jesus and have been changed by him. This is a massive demonstration of the truth of the resurrection. It is not a question of accepting one doctrine among many and defending it. It is a question of personal experience. All down the ages since the first century there have been hordes of people who, like Saul of Tarsus, have turned right round from being totally opposed or indifferent to Christianity, to being utterly convinced it is true. I guess you are one of them. I know I am.

The evidence for the resurrection is overwhelming. No wonder Theodore Momsen, one of the greatest classical historians, called the resurrection 'the best attested fact in ancient history'. Lord Darling, Lord Chief Justice of England some years ago, declared:

> We as Christians are asked to take a very great deal on trust: the teachings, for example, and the miracles of Jesus. If we had to take it all on trust I, for one, would be sceptical. The crux of the problem whether Jesus was or was not what he claimed to be must surely depend on the truth or otherwise of the resurrection. On that greatest point we are not merely asked to have faith. In its favour as a living truth there exists such overwhelming evidence, positive and negative, factual and circumstantial that no intelligent jury in the world could fail to bring in the verdict that the resurrection story is true.

The resurrection: a different perspective

The resurrection is one of the strongest cards in our pack. And it is so practical. It makes an enormous difference to the whole subject of death, and we need to be clear about it if we are to be of help to people.

It makes an enormous difference to *the fact of death*. Jesus, unlike Socrates, did not pretend that death was a friend. It was the Last Enemy. It is part of the fallenness of the world. It is the end result of human rebellion against God. That is why Jesus wept at Lazarus' tomb and sweated blood at the approach of his own death. But endure it he did – and what encouragement that gives us as we face it for ourselves. He understands. He has been through it. Moreover he conquered it. The resurrection shows that death does not have the last word in God's world. Everything is different since the first Easter.

And then it makes an enormous difference to *our approach to death*. The resurrection speaks to our fears:

'In my Father's house are many room; if it were not so, I would have told you. I am going there to prepare a place for you' (John 14:2, NIV). It speaks to our priorities. As Martin Luther King put it, 'Only that man is free who is not hung up on his own dying but lives as though death were dead.' Dr King certainly lived like that himself, and so may we. For death is a defeated foe. Christ has drawn its fangs. This should also make a difference to our affections. 'Set your minds on things that are above, not on things that are on earth,' the apostle tells us (Colossians 3:2). I read of a doctor who made a study of the junk people were reading just before death struck. They were foolishly rooted to this life, from which they were so soon to be taken. Contrast the Christian attitude as exemplified in the apostle Paul: 'For to me to live is Christ, and to die is gain' (Philippians 1:21).

The resurrection makes an enormous difference too to *bereavement*. Christians have the Lord's promise: 'Where I am you shall be also.' And that is worth a lot. We also have his people, that great family of believers, some at least of whom will take trouble in visiting and encouraging the bereaved. And best of all, we have the presence of the Risen One with us. He will accompany us along every stage of the journey until we reach the great reunion in heaven with those whose journey is already complete. At the end of the road, there is nothing to fear. That was the message of Maria, a Russian nun, to a terrified Jewish girl in Ravensbrück concentration camp. She walked voluntarily into the gas chamber alongside the condemned girl with an arm around her shoulder, saying, 'Christ is risen. There is nothing to fear.'

I have spent some time on this aspect of our journey, because every one of us is getting nearer death every day, and it is an important topic which our society generally sweeps under the carpet. It is important to have clear views on the future hope which Christianity offers, so that we can face our own aging, suffering and death with greater peace, we can encourage the bereaved, and we can help people who are agnostic about the whole subject to see the evidence on which they can make an informed decision. As the road sign says, 'Do not enter the box unless your exit is clear.'

I want to close this chapter about the journey with an excerpt from a personal letter I received recently. It was from a doctor and his wife whom I had known in their student days when I was a rector in Oxford. They wrote out of the blue:

> . . . thank you for the wonderful foundation your church has provided for us over the years. Your aim in student ministry was to turn out Christians equipped to go out and fight the

good fight in the world. And that is what has happened to us. Bill [not his real name] is currently engaged in research in San Francisco aimed at converting star wars technology into lasers which can help reduce abortions recommended for babies with cardiac defects, discovered on routine antenatal ultra-sounds. He must be doing something right, as 1997 has proved to be a year marked by some unemployment and unforeseen setbacks which are surely part of the spiritual battle. There were samples which were lost by the laboratory and yet mirac-ulously turned up just in time. There were visas which expired and meant we had to leave the US with two weeks' notice, and we got back just in time to apply for a million dollar grant to further the research. One month's pay cheque has somehow lasted six, even though we were dipping into savings every month before unemployment started. We are beginning to see deeper reasons why God healed Bill of cancer when he was an undergraduate, and pray that he will continue to protect us as Bill moves deeper into research and the world of medical ethics. God clearly needs Bill to speak out, and he never would have been prepared if God had not provided you as a guide back in 1981.

The Alpha course, like life as a whole of which it is a mini-ature, is all about process. It is a journey, a pilgrimage. You have started well. Keep going, hand in hand with Christ, even when there is little fellowship and the going is hard. He will see you through to the end.

4

The Transforming Friendship

If Christianity is Christ, then it is just as important to go on with him as it is to begin with him. One of the most amazing statements in the Bible is contained in the simple words of Jesus: 'No longer do I call you servants . . . I have called you friends' (John 15:15). Jesus, who shares God's very nature, who was God the Father's agent in creation, who is at once origin, sustainer and goal of the universe, is prepared to call us friends. Friends, when we have disobeyed him. Friends, when we have not wanted to know him. Friends, when we have been rebels. It is simply amazing.

Pie in the sky?

When we commit our lives to Christ we begin a life of friendship with him which is meant to go on and get richer until our dying day. And then we shall see him face to face, and it will be wonderful. The one I now know by faith I shall then see. The one I love fitfully, I shall then be united to for ever. 'In thy presence there is fullness of joy, in thy right hand are pleasures for evermore,' sang the psalmist (Psalm 16:11), and I believe it. The first instalment of life with Christ here on earth brings so much joy and fulfil-

73

ment that there is every reason to believe him when he promises that the climax of it all, after this life is over, will be infinitely satisfying. This means that I can see my life steadily and see it whole: as a friendship with Christ who will stick with me, change me, and in the end receive me into his presence.

Now notice two things about this Christian hope, to which we gave some attention in the previous chapter. It is not pie in the sky when you die. The pie, or a great slice of it, is available here and now as we enjoy the Lord's company day by day. It would be infinitely worth while even if this life were all there is. But Jesus has said that this life is not all there is, and he has backed up his words with the resurrection. I'm prepared to take his word for it. He has penetrated beyond the bounds of death. He knows.

Rewards and punishments?

Just as it isn't pie in the sky when you die, neither is it, as some maintain, a refined form of selfishness to look forward to heaven. I do not love my Lord Jesus because I fear hell (though I believe that without Christ hell is my portion). I do not love him because I want to go to heaven (I don't want to go if he is not there – endless existence without him would be tedious and boring in the extreme). I love him for himself. I love him because he went to the cross for me, and because he patiently waited until I was willing to make room in my crowded life for him. I love him because he is so patient with me, while I am such a poor follower. That is why I love him. The thought of reward and punishment does not play any significant part in my motivation as a Christian. I believe in heaven because Jesus taught it, and I trust him. If he says our friendship is too precious for him to scrap at death, that is good enough for me. It is wonderfully generous of him to be willing to go on sharing his new life with us for ever. But it is just like him, for his name is Love.

The supreme ambition

Yes, Christ is the friend who will receive us at the end of the journey, just as he was the friend who accepted us at the start. The Christian life begins and ends with him. It is significant that St Paul, who came to know Christ initially on the Damascus Road, should, a quarter of a century later, put us in the picture about the continuing ambition of his life: 'That I may know him' (Philippians 3:10). To know him! That was the very centre of Christian living for the great apostle. He knew Christ already, of course – as you do. He had known him for more than twenty-five years, in times of loneliness and success, elation and depression, in the banqueting hall and in the dungeon, on dry land and in shipwreck; and yet his aim was to know him better. Perhaps in that simple but profound ambition we have plumbed the innermost secret of the greatness of St Paul. Christ was his friend, and for that friend he was willing to work and suffer, come what may. But most of all he wanted to know Jesus better. He would have approved of the famous prayer of Richard of Chichester:

> Thanks be to thee, my Lord Jesus Christ,
> for all the benefits thou hast won for me,
> for all the pains and insults thou hast borne for me.
> O most merciful redeemer, friend and brother,
> may I know thee more clearly,
> love thee more dearly,
> and follow thee more nearly,
> for thy name's sake.

The phone and the letter

But how are we to develop that friendship with the Lord, especially when the weekly encouragement of Alpha is no more? How *can* you develop a relationship with someone you can't see?

There are basically two ways. Friends and lovers can keep in touch, when separated, by writing letters (including faxes and e-mails) and using the phone. You know how keenly you wait for a call from that man you love, or how enthusiastically you scan your e-mail post office or the letters that drop on the mat, in the hope that *she* has written. And you know what it is like when two lovers are on the phone and you are waiting to make a call!

It is like that with Christ. Before we came to know him we had no particular desire to get in touch, even if we believed in his existence. But now that we know him and love him, it is very different. We are keen to use the letter and the phone. It is no miserable rule that we have to keep in order to preserve the friendship. It is the most natural thing in the world for friends to do.

The Bible: God's open letter

Our Lord has in fact written an open letter to all members of his family. St Augustine, quite correctly, called the Bible 'letters from home'. In them God tells us about himself, about successes and failures of past members of the family, about the family lifestyle and about resources which are available to all members. There are promises to claim, commands to obey, advice to note, prayers to echo and examples to follow. You know about this. Perhaps you began the habit of Bible reading during your Alpha course. You know that, on a good day at least, this time of

Bible reading has thrilled your heart as it has brought you into close touch with your Lord. You agree with the claim of the Scriptures themselves that they function as food, without which we shall starve; as a sword, without which we shall be defeated; as a lamp to shed light on our path; as a mirror, for lack of which we shall fail to see what we really look like; as a fire to warm our cold hearts when they lose their glow; and as a hammer to break the rock in pieces when we are being wilfully disobedient. You know, though you may not always admit it, that you simply cannot afford to neglect the Scriptures if you want your relationship with the Lord to develop.

Inevitably, however, as you progress in the Christian life, you will find problems both in the area of Bible reading and of prayer. It is important to face them honestly, not least because if you keep your devotional life insulated from your reason, there is going to be a terrible explosion one day. You may even be shipwrecked and leave your Christianity behind, as some, sadly, have done. Here are a few of the issues you may have to face, and some suggestions towards an answer.

1. The church wrote the Bible, and the church is free to improve on it

That attitude is not uncommon, though it is not usually expressed as crudely as that. However, I noticed recently that this is precisely the position being advocated by the newly elected presiding bishop of the Episcopal Church in the USA. He publicly acknowledges that his church is formally in contradiction to the Bible, and is sanctioning practices forbidden in the Bible, but he maintains that the church nowadays has a deeper insight into the mind of Christ and this allows it to contradict the actual teaching Jesus gave in his day.

This sort of thing needs thinking through carefully, since it is likely to increase in the current permissive climate. The first response I would want to make is that we can only know the mind of Christ through what the Gospels and Epistles tell us. We have no independent access to him. And if our revisionist friends tell us, as they will, that the Holy Spirit is guiding them into new truth, we need to remember that not all development is healthy development. It can be very corrosive. After all, cancer is a kind of development! How are we to tell which 'developed' ideas should be accepted and which rejected? Jesus maintained that his words would never pass away (Mark 13:31). Are we to believe him, or those who say, quite shamelessly, that Jesus was wrong, while still professing to worship him?

Second, we need to remember that the early church never thought it was conferring authority on the particular books it gradually collected into the canon of the New Testament. The church already acknowledged the divine authority of the Old Testament, and it was seeking the authentic witness to Jesus written by apostles or 'apostolic men' to put alongside it. It differentiated sharply between the primary witness to Jesus given by the apostles and its own position in a later age. 'Christ is from God and the apostles from Christ,' wrote Clement of Rome about AD 95 (*Epistle*, 42). Ignatius, who was martyred about AD 115, wrote, 'I do not command you like Peter and Paul did. They were apostles. I ought rather to be schooled by you' (*Romans* 4). And in a famous passage to the Philadelphians (chapter 5) he puts the prophets, the apostles and the Gospels on the same authoritative level. Again Polycarp, writing about AD 116, says, 'Let us so serve Jesus with all reverence and fear as he has himself given us commandment, as did the apostles who preached the gospel to us, and the prophets who proclaimed beforehand the coming of the Lord' (*Polycarp*, 6). The subsequent church has always been acutely aware of the special place in God's revelation occupied by the prophets who looked forward to the coming of Jesus and the apostles who looked back on it. They did not find books coming from the apostolic circle and make them Scripture. They reverenced them because they *were* Scripture, and as such were there for Christian disciples down the ages to follow and obey, not to 'improve'.

2. The New Testament is late and unreliable

Nicky Gumbel has dealt admirably with this claim in his *Questions of Life,* the book of the Alpha course. Get it if you do not already have a copy, and read Chapter 2. It is no longer possible for any honest person to maintain that the New Testament was written long after the events there recorded, and that the text has been altered out of all recognition. For many decades this was the communist propaganda, and it is totally discredited. We have manuscripts of some parts of the New Testament from within fifty years of the originals, and that is mind-boggling in terms of ancient documents. Nobody doubts the substantial accuracy of the text of Herodotus and Thucydides, but the gap between the earliest extant copy and the autographs is some 1,300 years. With Caesar it is 950 years. We are in an incomparably better position with the New Testament, of which we have some 5,000 Greek manuscripts, 10,000 Latin and almost as many written in Armenian, Coptic and other ancient versions. The mass of early manuscripts and the extensive quotation of the New Testament in the writings of the second and third centuries give us grounds for rock-solid confidence in the reliability of the text of the New Testament. While there are

obviously slight verbal differences among all these manuscripts, there is no doubt at all that we have some 98 per
cent of the New Testament precisely as its authors wrote
it, and there is no way that major interpolations could
have been included into it. There is no doubt about the
text. Obeying it is a different matter!

3. What about the miracles in the New Testament?

I am not in the least inclined to discredit the New
Testament because the miraculous occurs on many of its
pages. The really massive miracles are the coming of God
into the world he made, and his resurrection from the dead.
The miracles of healing, feeding crowds of hungry people
and so forth are chicken feed compared to the incarnation
and resurrection. If the central claim of Christianity is
true, and God really has invaded our world in the person of
Jesus Christ, would you not expect the occasional ripple on
the surface of our pond to mark his presence? And remember, the miracles of Jesus are never for show. They are *acted
testimony* to who he is. Both his words and his deeds under-
line his claims. All three stand or fall together.

4. What about the parts of Scripture I find unacceptable?

I think we have to be very clear about this. There are only
three possible sources of authority in the Christian life.
God has given us the Bible, our reason and the teaching
tradition of the church down the ages. Clearly all three
have value. But to which shall we assign priority when
there is a clash?

Shall we rely on tradition? Tradition can easily depart
from the original standard of Jesus. He pointed that out
in his own day: the main religious teachers, the Pharisees,
had actually rejected the word of God in order to maintain their tradition (Mark 7:9).

Or shall we rely on our very limited reason to decide all our problems about God? The Sadducees took that line in Jesus' day, maintaining that there was no possibility of life after death: when you're dead, you're dead. Jesus rebuked them for both their unbelief and their ignorance of the Scriptures (Matthew 22:23–33). It was to the Scriptures that he always resorted in order to determine doubtful issues, and we would do well to follow his example if we are his disciples – even when we find it hard.

I was listening only last night to a bishop who had lost both wife and son to cancer within a few months. He was devastated. He could not eat properly, pray, or read the Scriptures for ages. He felt God had savaged him. He wondered if God even existed. But he came to a place where he saw that God was calling him to repent of his doubts and trust him fully, even though he could not understand him.

He did just that, and you should see him now. He is confi-dent, full of joy and love, and fearless as he faces a lonely future. Faith is not blind, but it recognises how limited its understanding is. The Christian who can say, 'I do not fully understand you, but I trust you,' is not committing intellectual suicide, but is discovering the pathway to mature discipleship, for God has a way of humbling the proud and revealing himself to the humble.

We would do well to recognise that there are bound to be things about God and his ways that we do not under-stand, and to concentrate on doing the things that we can understand. Meanwhile, why not keep a list of problems that bother you? More experienced Christians may well be able to help. And when you come up against the most inscrutable problems, take heart. They will have exer-cised lots of Christian thinkers before you, and there is sure to be some helpful book on the problem for you to read.

There are many such difficulties you will encounter in the Bible. The important thing is not to allow them to stop you from reading it. You will find it is indispensable for healthy growth in your relationship with Christ.

Bible reading – a new legalism?

Does it seem that I am legislating? As if being a Christian involves a set of rules, one of which is: 'Read your Bible every day'? That is not the case. There is no rule about it. But it stands to reason that if you love someone you will want to explore them fully, and if you can't see them but they communicate by letter or e-mail, then you don't find it any hardship to read the letters! Sometimes Christians have made a fetish of Bible reading. They have implied that unless you read it daily, and preferably before breakfast, you are going to make a mess of the day and betray Christ.

There is a general reaction in Christian circles these days against such legalism, and rightly so. Jesus is not so mean as to withdraw his friendship if we skip Bible reading for a day, or two, or three. But if it is true that the Bible is one of the main sources of nourishment for the Christian (and it is), then ask yourself how well you would grow physically if you ate your meals at rare and irregular intervals. If you are no good in the mornings, read it at night. But I can't help reflecting that most great men and women of God in the past have found that if they did not make time for Bible reading and prayer at the start of the day (for however short a time) they didn't make time at all. You may be different. You may be iron-willed. You may be a busy young mother who can only get alone for half an hour when your husband has gone to work and you have done the school run. You may be a night-owl, who can guard that last half-hour of the day for God. Find a time that suits you, and keep it special. The important thing is for you to meet your Lord, not when or where you do it, or how long you spend at it.

Ringing the changes

You will already have made a start at reading the Bible devotionally. Many people find the Bible Reading Fellowship notes, Scripture Union notes or *Every Day with Jesus* helpful aids for regular, practical Bible reading. In each of them you are given the passage for the day, some brief and helpful comment on it, and a suggested prayer. Such systems generally guide the reader through one of the biblical books.

I myself begin with a prayer that God will shine his light

on the page I am about to read. Then I read it through
slowly, looking for something striking. It may be an insight
about God I have never seen before. It may be an encouragement. It may be a command or a warning. Sometimes
it is a prayer I can use for myself and my friends. I take my
time. I often have a pen and paper handy. And I pause to
meditate over suggestive phrases and try to apply them to
my own life. This leads naturally into prayer.

Such is my general pattern, but I am not afraid to
change it when I need some variety. Why not branch out
on your own? Sometimes you might read a whole book in
one sitting: the book of Jonah, for example, if you are
feeling a bit rebellious; or Peter's first letter if you are going
through a tough time at work. Sometimes you might meditate on a single verse. For instance, John 3:16, the most
famous verse in the whole Bible, tells us of our great need:
we are perishing, like someone drowning in a river. It
speaks of God's great love: he gave Jesus to meet that profound human need. And it speaks of a step of faith
whereby all who believe in him may taste God's new life
for themselves. By the time you have dug deep into a verse
like that you may find you have learned it by heart, and
that can prove very useful to you later on when you are
trying to help someone else.

There are lots of other ways to study the Bible. You can
do a character study, and trace the references in the New
Testament to a man like Andrew. He is mentioned only
three times outside the list of disciples, but on each occasion he is introducing someone else to Jesus. Or take one
of the great heroes of faith in the Old Testament, such as
Abraham, and see how he faced the inducement to take
the easy course for fear of appearing odd, and his temptations to selfishness, to self-pity and to water down God's
promises. That man faced the same difficulties as we do,

and yet he learned to trust God deeply in them. His example can go a long way to inspire and teach us today.

Alternatively, you can study a theme: what the Bible has to say about work, money, marriage, parenting, faith and so forth. You will need a concordance, which tabulates the occurrence of words in the Bible, but they are easy to find in good bookstores and can now be obtained on disk. As a change, you could take a single chapter and see what its main teaching is. Romans 8 is a great chapter, with its assurance about a Christian's past, present and future with Christ. So is 2 Timothy 2, with its seven distinct pen portraits of a Christian worker. Or you can trace a single significant word, such as 'inheritance', 'faithful' or 'able'. I have discovered a great deal by investigating the Christian inheritance which God has provided, by considering where he is calling me to be faithful, and by reflecting on what he has pledged himself able to do in me and through me.

Going deeper

These are some of the different ways in which you can approach that inexhaustible book, the Bible. But I fancy you may find yourself being drawn in even deeper, in a number of ways.

First, you will want to read the Bible with attention to the circumstances in which it arose. These differ widely. It consists, after all, of sixty-six books written in three languages over a period of more than a thousand years. So you will want to get hold of a good commentary to see the book you are studying against its background. William Barclay's commentaries cover the whole New Testament, are highly readable, generally reliable, and full of fascinating insights. The Tyndale commentaries have proved themselves very valuable, and Dr John Stott has edited *The*

Bible Speaks Today, a series of commentaries which combine honest biblical exposition with sharp contemporary application.

Second, you will probably want to read the Bible with others. You may already have done that in the Alpha course. There is tremendous value in sitting with a group of friends and studying a passage together, each of you sharing your insights and building one another up. Why not join such a group if there is one in your church? If not, perhaps you and a friend could get together and start one? You may be surprised at the number of people who would like to share in something like this once they hear it is available. You may not feel you could offer leadership in such a group by yourself, but that doesn't matter. Share the leadership out among the members of the group, so that everyone has a go. After all, it is not as if you were being asked to preach a sermon. It is merely to chair the discussion for one evening among a group of friends. That could provide a marvellous means of growth for the people concerned.

I was talking recently with George Gallup, the president of the famous Gallup Polls, and he told me what he did when he had the idea of a group like this. He called up twelve men he knew and invited them. Ten of them said 'yes' and that began the small group involvement which has become a tremendous enrichment of his life for many years. It could be the same for you.

Third, why not read the Bible with a friend? I mentioned before that in the early days of my own discipleship, a friend sat down with me once a week for a few months to get me started. He would choose an appropriate passage and we would ask God to guide us. Then we would read it through, share our insights and pray about them. He would help me with problems I was experiencing in my Christian life, and I would go on my way enormously encouraged. You could do that with a friend of yours, could you not? It would be a marvellous way of investing what you have learned from Alpha in another person's life.

Fourth, it is a tremendous help to go to a conference to deepen your Christian life. There are many such available, often combined with a holiday element. New Wine, Spring Harvest and the Keswick Convention readily come to mind, but there are many more. To spend some of your vacation time not only with the family, if you have one, but in the company of many other Christians all seeking to deepen their understanding and practice of the Christian life is very enriching.

The essential attitude

But however we read the Bible, let us not forget the right approach if we want our spiritual lives to grow. It is not a case of 'the Bible as literature', or 'the Bible as history', but rather 'the Bible as God's loving letter to you'. Come to it determined to make contact with him. And make sure that your Bible reading is not one-way traffic. You will often want to pause and give thanks for some new insight, respond to some new challenge or search your conscience in response to what you have read. Bible reading, in fact, leads naturally into prayer. Reading the Lord's letter drives you to pick up the phone of prayer.

I once asked a student who had come to Christ only a month earlier, 'What is the greatest difference you have noticed?' Her reply was interesting: 'I have begun to love praying. I sometimes go on for ages, because I am really in touch.' That girl had learned the meaning of prayer. It is talking with God. Talking with him about anything and everything of concern to us: friends, the job, time off, home relationships, career, disappointments, joys, every-

thing – especially the day's programme. Prayer is assuredly
not a matter of set words (though formal prayers may have
a proper place in a church service so that all present can
join in) nor of fixed times (though without fixed times our
praying will become spasmodic and probably chaotic). It
is the sharing of our whole life with the one we love. Why
do you think Christ died? To show us his love? Yes. To take
responsibility for our sins? Yes. But supremely in order to
share our life with us. '[He] died for us so that whether we
wake or sleep we might live with him' (1 Thessalonians
5:10). Yes, *live with him,* with all the barriers formed by
unforgiven sin broken down, and with nothing between us
to spoil the friendship.

The phone of prayer

The following letter came to me from a young woman who
had been a dancer, a model, a nanny, and has subsequently
married a clergyman. When she wrote it she had only been
a Christian for a few months, and this is what prayer was
beginning to mean to her:

> When I pray, it is to get close to God, to thank him for all he
> has done for me and to praise him for his glory. To ask for
> strength to do his will so that through my actions people will
> see him in me. To get so close in the quietness of the mind that
> God can tell me what he wants me to do for him. To ask help
> for myself and all my friends and family, and for this world
> and its sin. To ask for forgiveness, and strength not to sin
> again. To talk quietly with my Friend and my God and tell him
> all my inner feelings that I could never share with anyone else.

That is the essence of prayer: sharing everything with
God. It means talking with him, and it means listening to
him too. We are not very good at this – at least I'm not. I
tend to talk too much, and that makes it hard for him to

show me his will. Perhaps you are much the same – so busy talking down the phone of prayer that you don't realise he is trying to get through to you! Perhaps he wants you to call on that lonely person down the road, to take a bag of fruit to that person you know in the mental hospital, or not to be impatient with your children. Perhaps there is a gift of money he wants you to part with, or a word of encouragement for the person working alongside you in the job. As long as you will give him the chance, by making time to listen to him, it is up to him to get through to you, is it not? I find that comforting. It is his responsibility to show me his will. It is mine to do it.

You have already made an initial study of prayer in the Alpha course (Chapter 6 of *Questions of Life*). There Nicky Gumbel examined what prayer is and why it is so important. He wrote about the painful experience we all go through when prayers are not answered as we would wish, and he took us helpfully through the Lord's Prayer as a model for our own intercessions. Let's go a little further.

The power of intercession

Jesus told us to ask, to seek and to knock. All Christians know that this brings results, at least sometimes. We do not know how prayer works, but it does. Prayer is not battering the ear of a reluctant God. It is coming to the heavenly Father as children who have been adopted into his family and have concerns on our hearts. What good father refuses to listen to his children? It is not surprising, then, that the Bible is full of encouragements to pray. We can be confident of a sympathetic hearing.

Neither is prayer attempting to change God's mind – to twist his arm, so to speak. It is not, as the old saying has it, 'moving the hand that moves the world'. It is, rather, co-operating with him in his purposes for good. He could no doubt bring them to fruition without us, but he has chosen to do so with our co-operation. I lack the wisdom to know what is best, and I lack the ability to bring it about, but I come humbly to the one who has both wisdom and power, and I seek to be available to him. Sometimes that availability will entail action on my part. Sometimes it will mean leaving the prayers with him and trusting him for the outcome.

It is important to realise that not even God can always bring about what we pray for. Just as he has limited himself to seek our co-operation, so he has limited himself by entrusting us human beings with free will. Without it we would be mere robots, programmed to perform, and that would never satisfy the God who is love. But if he has given us free will, he cannot force himself upon us, or upon those for whom we pray. He will not do it; that would make us less than human. So although God in his love and generosity woos and cajoles the hearts of people who have no time for him, he will not force them. A mother's prayers for her wayward son are no guarantee of his return – he has free will. Yet many will testify to the way their rebellion has been broken down by the prayers of a loved one. I often ask new Christians who has been praying for them, and they generally know! You probably know the classic story of the young Augustine, the brilliant intellectual and passionate sensualist, who came to faith after thirty years of his mother's prayers. When he burst into the house to tell of his spectacular conversion, he found her on her knees, praying for him. That story has been repeated in countless lives. Prayer alters things – it is part of God's chemistry of change.

How important, then, to pray for others – our nearest and dearest, those we find it hard to like, our employers and workmates, and the names that God's Holy Spirit puts on our hearts. It's a remarkable thing, but the Holy Spirit will from time to time almost burden us with a name or two, when we should be praying for them. And sometimes we will discover, subsequently, that at the very moment we were praying the person concerned was affected for good. That happened to my son when he was cycling from Vancouver to Buenos Aires. As he went down the waterless wastes of the Baja Desert, he was twice nearly killed, and on each occasion he was aware that others were praying for him, at that moment.

I heard of a most extreme example of something similar more recently. A medical missionary was reporting back to his home church in Michigan in 1997. He told how, while serving a small field hospital in Africa, he travelled regularly through the jungle to a nearby town for supplies. This entailed camping halfway overnight. Once, on returning from the town with fresh supplies, he found two men fighting, one of whom was badly hurt. He treated him and spoke to him of Christ. That night he camped in the jungle, and returned to his hospital without incident. Days later the man he had treated sought him out and said, 'We realised you carried money and medicine. So some friends and I followed you into the jungle, knowing you would camp overnight. We planned to kill you and take your money and drugs. Just as we were about to move into your campsite we saw the twenty-six armed guards you had around you.' The missionary doctor laughed, 'I had no guards. I was quite alone.' The young man pressed the point. 'No, sir. I was not the only one who saw the guards. My five friends all saw them and counted them. It was because of those guards that we left you alone.'

At this point in the church presentation in Michigan, a man jumped up and asked the missionary, 'Can you tell me the exact date when this happened?' The missionary thought for a moment and then recalled the date. The man in the congregation then explained, 'On that night in Africa it was morning here. I was preparing to play golf. As I put my bag in the car, I felt the Lord leading me to pray for you. In fact, the urge was so strong that I called some of the men of the church together to pray for you. Will all those men who met with me that day please stand up?' They stood. There were twenty-six of them!

That is what intercession inspired by God's Spirit can do.

Corporate prayer

Recognising the power of intercession may lead you to start praying with other people. There are many ways in which you can do this. One is to become part of a small group of friends who support each other in prayer. My wife and I belong to a group like that. We have lunch together, then we feed each other news and needs, and we pray. Not only then, but we try to pray regularly for each other's needs and engagements until we meet again a month later. I am often asked how my joy and energy are maintained. The answer is, of course, from God, but that praying circle of friends has a lot to do with it!

A second obvious example of corporate prayer is the prayer team. Many churches recognise the gifts of intercession among some of their members and get them together into a team to pray for specific needs and people. Sometimes, of course, these intercessors are older people or those who are housebound, but not necessarily. The prayer team is generally available after services to pray with people who so desire. Before long it becomes very natural for members of the congregation to go to them with prayer requests, and then to depart encouraged. A burden shared is so often a burden halved.

A third example of corporate prayer is the phonelink. A need is disclosed to one of the intercessors in a church and they immediately ring up another person on the chain, who rings the next and so on. Soon there is intensive prayer throughout the circle for the need in question, although the people are in different places. A worldwide group of women, the Lydia Fellowship, has offered this gift of intercession to the wider church in this way, but many local churches have prayer chains that you can link into.

If Alpha has led you into a new vitality in prayer, might

God not be calling you to start engaging in some such corporate prayer for other people?

Spiritual battle

This leads me to say something about spiritual battle. It is an almost universal experience that when we wake up to the reality and power of the Holy Spirit we become increasingly and uncomfortably aware of the reality and power of an unholy spirit. In Ephesians 6:10ff. Paul encourages us to put on the whole armour of God, so that we may be able to stand against all the wiles of the devil. He reminds us that we are not merely fighting 'against flesh and blood, but against the principalities, against the powers, against the world rulers of this present darkness, against the spiritual hosts of wickedness in the heavenly places'. And the ultimate weapon he encourages us to take up is prayer: 'Pray at all times in the Spirit, with all prayer and supplication . . . for all the saints, and also for me.'

In other words, there is a spiritual battle between the forces of God and Satan, and prayer is the way to win. I do not want to over-dramatise the spiritual battle, but neither do I want to minimise its importance. Many Christians go through their whole lives without realising the battle is on. It is not surprising that they are ineffective. The book of Acts shows how seriously the first Christians took this spiritual battle. The apostles Peter and John emerge from the first of their imprisonments, and what do they and their colleagues do? They pray to the 'Sovereign Lord, who didst make the heaven and the earth' and call upon him to look on the threats of their persecutors and do whatever he saw to be best about it (Acts 4:23ff.). Or think of when Peter was thrown into prison again by the tyrannical King Herod Agrippa. We read, 'So Peter was kept in prison; but earnest prayer for him was made to God by the church' (Acts 12:1–5). And, to their amazement, Peter escaped.

Often prayer is intensified by fasting (see Acts 13:2–3). This is the deliberate abstinence from some normal feature of life, be it food, sleep, sex, or in our own day TV, in order to prioritise prayer at a time when the intensity of the spiritual battle demands serious commitment. I fancy that if we took this dimension of the Christian life more seriously we would see the Christian cause advance more speedily and strongly. That is certainly what they found in Eastern Europe under communist rule. Oppression was defeated by prayer and fasting.

Contemplation

But there is another side to prayer, where more introverted Christians have much to teach their activist friends. It is the constructive use of silence. There are times when we need to retreat into the inner core of our being along with the Holy Spirit of God who lives within us. We get past asking for anything, past worrying about anything, even past praise and thanksgiving. The mud in our lives slowly sinks to the bottom, and through the clear water we get to contemplate the Lord himself, in all his beauty and attractiveness. We revel in his love. We adore him for who he is. For some it may take only a few minutes to reach this level of prayer. For others it may take an hour or more. But if we give time and priority to this dimension of prayer we will be doing what we were made for, and will return to the hurly-burly of daily life renewed and refreshed.

Many people these days have turned to Eastern meditation as a refuge from the strains and stresses of life. This may look much the same as Christian contemplation, but in reality it is utterly different. They seek independence; we seek deeper dependence. They seek self-realisation and fulfilment; we seek God's Holy Spirit to renew us. They relate to their inner core; we relate to the living God. And our lives should show the difference. This quiet, adoring waiting upon God is much stronger in Catholic and Orthodox branches of Christianity than it is among Evangelicals and charismatics. None of us is complete in the Christian tradition in which we have been raised. We all need to learn from each other.

Many Christians of all traditions find the Jesus Prayer an enormous help in contemplating the Lord and getting soaked in him. It is short and simple: 'Lord Jesus Christ, Son of God, have mercy on me.' Bishop Simon Barrington-Ward has written a most helpful short book on this prayer, entitled simply *The Jesus Prayer*. In it he tells of a period of great pressure in his own life when he was travelling for the Church Missionary Society in Africa and Asia. He found himself in an Orthodox monastery one day and heard them praying, 'Lord Jesus Christ, Son of God, have mercy on me.' He relates what followed: 'There was a pause. And then the prayer was repeated. We were lifted up into the steady wingbeat of the prayer. As we settled into it and began to be drawn into it, we felt the whole focus of whole community and of our own beings.' He went on:

> Our mind could wander – and we could even go to sleep. Yet all the time the prayer was going on, and we were part of it. The constant repetition of the words 'Lord Jesus Christ' kept on recalling us to the presence. And the constant movement of the prayer, 'have mercy on me', was something that immediately began to grasp me very deeply. After I came out of the chapel the prayer was still praying itself within me for many hours.

You might find this a real help in your own prayers. It has a profundity and simplicity which leads many deep into the presence of the Lord. It can be an individual or corporate form of contemplating the reality and mercy of the Lord we love.

Retreats

Increasingly people are making for monasteries and retreat houses for a day, a weekend, or for longer periods of withdrawal. This is surprising in view of the declining numbers of monks and nuns, and the secularisation of our culture. And yet it is not so surprising. The massive pressures of everyday life drive us to seek solitude, a place apart, where we can just *be*. And Christians will want to just be – with God. Often it helps to have a 'soul friend' or spiritual director, who can help you to make the most of a time like this, guide your reading, strengthen your spiritual discipline, and help you conduct a spiritual MOT on your life. Most of the Christian leaders I respect do have a spiritual director who is wise, utterly confidential, and with whom they can share weaknesses, sins and fears. Most of the Christian leaders I respect have an extended time of retreat at least once a year, so as to draw closer to God, revel in his love, rediscover direction and priorities, and generally have their spiritual batteries recharged. If you would value a time of renewal like this, be it long or short, take a look at the list of religious houses, monasteries and retreat centres set out in the *Church of England Yearbook* or some similar book. Take the plunge and fix something up. You won't regret it.

Back to basics

Prayer is a growing relationship, and we will never fully plumb its depths this side of heaven. As we develop our prayer life, let us never feel that we have outgrown the basis of it all, the phone and the letter. We are, above all, asked by Jesus to abide in him like the branch in the vine. So do not limit your prayer life to special times, but turn to him at odd moments throughout the day. If you have just enjoyed an especially nice meal, say, 'Thank you, Lord' – and there's no need to shut your eyes and kneel down in order to say it. Does some pressing temptation attack you? Then say, 'Lord, please give me your strength.' Have you let him down? Don't wait until evening to put it right. Tell him at once: 'Lord, I've let you down. I am so sorry. Please forgive me, and help me to learn from my mistake, so that next time when I am tempted I will ask your help in good time.'

One final thing. Friendship is all the more delightful when shared. If you are out for the evening with some other Christians, why not spend a few minutes in prayer together before you go home? Break the sound barrier, launch out and it will be a blessing to you. I think I get as deep a level of fellowship with other Christians when praying briefly and informally with them like this at the end of an evening, as I ever do.

There it is then. Christ is not only our God but our Friend. And friendships need to be cultivated. Make sure yours does not fall into disrepair through neglect. The letter and the phone are indispensable for absent friends if they are to keep in touch. And though this analogy is not exact (Christ is not absent – by his Spirit he is with us all the time), nevertheless the point holds good. You and I must keep in touch with him and he with you, and the Bible and prayer are prime ways to do it.

5

The New Community

If you have been on an Alpha course, you will have had your eyes opened to a number of issues, but none more revolutionary than the subject of the church.

Misunderstandings

If you ask almost anyone where St Michael's Church is, they will direct you to a building. The church is *never* a building in the New Testament! Alpha, with its accent on Christian fellowship, will have made the biblical teaching very clear to you, that the church is not a building, but people. The building is the meeting place of God's people, and however old and precious (or shiny new) it may be, it is no more than that.

Another major misunderstanding is that the church means the clergy. 'Are you going into the church?' they ask you, when you let on that you may be considering ordination. But that is miles away from the teaching of the New Testament, where *all* Christians are members of the church. Indeed, there is no suspicion of that two-tier Christianity which is a trap into which almost all denominations have fallen. The sharp distinction between priest and people, ordained and lay, is remarkable for its absence in the pages of the New Testament.

Clergy and laity

This fact caused widespread amazement in the early days of the church. This was the first religion known to mankind which did not have a professional priesthood with sacrifices and altars. A Christian leader like Minucius Felix, writing in the middle of the second century, could say, 'We have no temples, no priests, no altars.' The reason was simple but revolutionary: all Christians were God's *laos,* his people, and all were his *kleros,* his clergy! This was no playing with words. It was making an important point that still needs stressing today, because it is so often overlooked. Christianity is a one-class faith. Nobody is higher up the pecking order than anyone else. Everyone is so precious to God that he has made us members of his very family, at the immense cost of the cross. You can't show greater love than that.

But equally the New Testament assures us that we are all God's *kleros*, his inheritance. Isn't that amazing? Had you ever imagined in your wildest dreams that God Almighty would count you part of his inheritance? Not just the clergy, as we call them, but all Christians without distinction – you included!

But the revolution cuts deeper. Most faiths have a special priesthood to take care of the people's relation to God. The priest speaks to people on God's behalf. And the priest prays for people and facilitates access to God for them. He is essentially the bridge-builder. The Latin word for that is *pontifex*, and it is a title the pope uses for himself as 'pontiff'. Strictly speaking, however, that title belongs to Jesus alone. He alone spans the gulf that yawns between God and man, because he alone is both God and man. And so we find the New Testament writers being very careful of their use of language. They are clear that Jesus alone is the supreme high priest (much of the central part of the letter to the Hebrews is concerned to establish that fact). Jesus is the one and only sacrificing priest (*hiereus*), who builds the bridge between God and mortal men. The Old Testament priests with their blood sacrifices pointed forward to Jesus, who would be both priest and sacrifice himself. He fulfilled it all and, as old Archbishop Cranmer put it, 'therein he hath neither partner nor successor'. Yes, the bridge-building job has been achieved, once and for all, through his death upon the cross, and it never needs to be repeated or supplemented. So we never find the New Testament writers calling a Christian leader a *hiereus,* a priest. They kept that name for Jesus. A collateral form of the word, *hierateuma,* is however applied to the whole Christian church (1 Peter 2:5, 9). The entire community of believers is called, in this derived sense, to do the two things the Old Testament priest did: bring the world to God in prayer, and bring God to the world in witness and service. Maybe you will have heard of the priesthood of all believers. This is what it means. The supreme high priest, Jesus, who has brought God to man fully in the incarnation, and man to God fully through the cross, entrusts to all of us the task and the inestimable privilege of representing mankind to God in prayer, and God to mankind in mission and service. He has made us a kingdom and priests to God (Revelation 1:6). This is for *all* Christians, not some. Isn't that a privilege?

While it is true that the New Testament never calls Christian leaders priests (and the English word 'priest' derives, in any case, not from the 'sacrificing priest' of antiquity but from the Greek *presbuteros*, 'elder'), it is strong on the need for leadership. Leadership is a special farewell gift of the ascended Christ to his church, and we need to respect it. There is some important teaching on the

subject in Ephesians 4:7–14, 1 Thessalonians 5:12–13 and
Hebrews 12:7, 17. Those references are worth looking up
and reflecting on. God cares about leadership, and the
ordained leadership in a church is very important.
Nevertheless, it cannot be equated with the church itself,
for the church is the body of Christ, and we all have a vital
part to play in that.

The body of Christ

An amazing picture

One of the most striking images of the Christian community, and one which dominates the New Testament, is the
mind-boggling idea that the church is the 'body of Christ'.
It is central to the understanding of the nature of the
church in Romans 12, 1 Corinthians 12, Ephesians chapters 1–2 and 4–5 and Colossians chapters 1–3. In these
latter references there is an added refinement to the image:
the ascended Christ is the head of the body. For as our
head embodies the brain, which is both the source of our
life and the organ which directs it, so Christ is both the
source of the church's life and its rightful director. Our
proper attitude is to respond to him, just as the limbs in
our own bodies respond to the brain directing them.

Think about it for a moment, and you will see what a
profound analogy this is. Just as you can only see what my
brain is thinking by the reaction of my body, so folk can
only discern the Christ they cannot see through the
actions of his people. They will inevitably judge him by us.
What an awesome responsibility!

And just as our limbs are all different, and have diverse
though complementary functions, so it is in the body of
Christ. We are all very different. The good Lord deliberately made us that way. We have different gifts, different

interests, and we need to co-ordinate them for the body's health and effectiveness – not to compete with one another, which is a failing you will often observe in church and society alike. Hence the vital importance of Christian unity and co-operation.

It stands to reason that if one part of our body gets enlarged out of all proportion, or another part gets paralysed, then the whole body is in trouble. So it is with the body of Christ. When some Christians puff themselves up and make out they are indispensable, or when other Christians simply do not pull their weight, the whole body suffers badly. And if arthritis sets in, and bone grates against bone rather than against the pad of gristle, the result is painful and the body becomes largely ineffective. Well, it's like that in the Christian body when members abandon the gristle of love, and argue and squabble among themselves. Above all, our bodies are designed to express the intention of the brain and do its bidding. Christ's body is intended to do precisely the same.

We can learn some crucial lessons about the Christian community from this brilliant image of the body. First, we see that every limb needs to be directly joined to Christ, otherwise it may look as if it belongs to his body, but in reality it will be like a glass eye or a false leg. It all begins with that personal commitment to him. It's vital.

Second, this image makes it clear that we all have different gifts, and we shall be accountable for their use to the Lord who gave them. Don't you dare insult your Maker by complaining, 'I don't have any gifts.' You have. It is your responsibility, perhaps with the help of others, to discover them and use them for him.

Third, we learn that we are not independent operators any more than the limbs of our body are. We depend on each other and operate well only if we are co-operating with each other. How we need to learn this lesson, particularly in the West where individualism runs riot.

Fourth, this simile reminds us that, like the limbs of our body, we have a job to do for Christ. Everyone is a minister, or 'servant' as the word really means, of Christ. You simply can't be a Christian without having a ministry of some sort.

Fifth, we see that the impact of the whole body is far greater than any one of its parts. This is yet another fruit of partnership and co-operation which is so essential. No wonder Jesus made it a priority for his followers.

Finally, 1 Corinthians 12 makes it plain that no jobs or talents are higher or more important than others in the Christian scene. God made all the limbs and set them in the body, endowing them with abilities as he thought fit.

The body working properly

I am writing this abroad while I am currently involved in the life of an amazing church. It is situated in the back of beyond, but hundreds of people are drawn to it from all over the surrounding area, because it embodies so much of what it means to be the body of Christ. It is a seven-day-a-week enterprise. Something is going on all the time. The lonely are loved into fellowship, the hungry are fed, visitors are warmly welcomed. The lifestyle of one and all of its members is dominated by the desire to serve the Christ they love by serving and loving other people. It shows, and it is mighty attractive. The event I have been involved in is just one of the many training weeks they offer, to share with other churches the principles of discipleship they have learned. Some 150 guests have fed in the church dining rooms on outstanding food cooked and served by volunteers, many of them retired. They have been housed and transported. There is an intensive programme of worship, lectures, discussion and seminars to suit a variety of tastes. Well over 100 of the church members have been involved in putting on this programme. They are the products of splendid, rich biblical teaching; they are strong, holy and well-informed disciples of Jesus. The church is permeated by small groups in which many broken people find new life and hope. The leadership, both of the church and of the groups, is shared; the preaching is powerful, the adult Sunday school is well attended, relevant and clear. The giving is massive and joyful, the missionary involvement (both long- and short-term) considerable. Everyone in the vicinity knows about the church, and new people join every week.

While the training course has been going on, scores more of the church have been involved in an alternative – and risky – programme. They have gone down to a large centre of population some miles away, and have had a week of talking to anyone they met about Jesus and the difference he makes to life. They have invited them back to a central secular venue where a free dinner is served and then a programme offered which is an imaginative introduction to Jesus Christ. One of the big stores has allowed them to sing daily inside the shop, and to speak to customers about their faith. People have been favourably surprised and impressed by this venture. It is so unusual. It gives, and asks for nothing in return – just like the gospel which it proclaims. It is centred around food and relaxed conversation at the table. It is a sharing of personal experience by the different limbs in Christ's body as they meet people on the street and call down God's peace and blessing upon them. It is transdenominational, as young and old combine in the ministry of drama, music, testimony and proclamation. It does not attempt to suck people into the church (as building and institution) in the first instance, but rather to bring the church (as people) to them. They are quite literally turning church inside out – getting the churchpeople out of their buildings and into the streets, with joy in their hearts and a word of witness and invitation on their lips. Need I add that people have become Christians this week who were totally outside any Christian influence a week ago? And what will happen to them now? They will be fed (surprise, surprise!) into an Alpha course.

The small group

Cells of life

All of this brings us to consider the vital importance of the small group in the life of the Christian community. It may be based in the home or the office or almost anywhere convenient. Nearly all the lively churches in the world depend to a considerable degree on the vitality of their small groups, and you who have spent three months and more in

such a group with Alpha need no persuasion of its importance. You therefore have a great deal to offer. You have hit
on a vital principle for the health and growth of the
church. We tend to be blind to its value before we join such
a group. Afterwards, it seems the most obvious thing in the
world. For it is here that you can develop quality relationships. It is here that you can be loved and encouraged.
Here is a group of people who, like you, are struggling
with issues of discipleship. You need each other.

So how can you apply this life-giving principle of the
small group to the local church?

Options

First, as we suggested earlier, you may find it helpful to go
through Alpha again, though it would be a pity if the
freshness of Alpha was diminished by the presence of lots
of old-timers! But if it was all very new to you, you may
find that some things you missed out on or failed to grasp
the first time become clear, and you will get a much better
idea of how the whole thing works and why it is so helpful.
Moreover, your presence will be a real help to the leaders,
and an encouragement to people joining the course for the
first time, who are, perhaps, either not yet Christians or
are unsure of where they stand. There's something to be
said for doing it twice.

Second, you may well be asked to help organise a fresh
Alpha. Perhaps you have secretarial skills. Perhaps you
love cooking. Perhaps you are happy to prepare rooms for
an event and clear up afterwards. Perhaps you have the
ability to give a talk clearly, humorously and in nonchurchy language. Maybe you have a talent for guiding
discussion. Maybe you have strong relational gifts with a
natural talent for one-to-one conversations. Maybe you
are good at none of these, but are brilliant at washing the

dishes. (I know I have four main talents, and one of them is washing-up!) There is room for a great deal of involvement and a wide variety of gifts in putting on an Alpha course really well. And the person who vacuums the floor is just as important as the person who gives the talk. The point is that Christ's body is working together harmoniously for the good of others. It is wildly attractive.

But what if there is no further Alpha in your church? Or what if there is, but you are not involved? Surely this is the ideal moment to talk things over with your vicar or pastor and mobilise a small group in your home. There will be a ready supply of people to join it, because others around you will have gone through one or more Alphas and be at a loose end. And if the reader of these pages happens to be a pastor, unsure of how to make the best use of those people in the congregation who have sprung into new life through Alpha, this is an opportunity too good to miss. It is the right time to start one or two home groups which in due time may spread into a network embracing most, if not all, of the congregation.

Fears and visions

Some clergy are sceptical of small groups. They feel that they might breed dissent. They might show an unwelcome independence. They might become a threat to the minister. I do not believe these fears are well grounded, though many clergy share them. If you, as a minister, will encourage such groups, see that wise leaders are put in place, and then take pains to support them in the basic pastoral work which will inevitably come their way, you will find the life of the parish greatly enriched. It will be a marvellously fruitful investment of time and effort – particularly if you meet up with the leaders on a regular basis. Suppose you have an evening with them every three months or so, it will enable them to share problems, to sharpen vision, to see the way ahead for the next period of the group's life – all in the course of frank discussion with their pastor.

I do not *think* this works. I know it does. I have had the joy of leading a large church with many such groups in it. I used to meet the leaders regularly, and one of our staff team offered constant support to them. We produced study material centrally, which the groups were free to use or not as they wished. We trusted the group leaders to lead, and the clergy only went into a group when invited. It was wonderful to see people developing gifts in ministry and the confidence to use them. Newcomers to the church first spent a few weeks in a welcoming group especially designed for the newly attached, and then were channelled into an appropriate home group. I found that these groups provided the close bonds of relationship which membership of a large congregation could not offer in its main services. In time they also became task forces to handle various needs which arose in the life of the church – be that help to resettle an evicted family, to decorate part of the church for Christmas, to put on a meal for street people, to serve coffee or lunch after the service, or to go away together on an evangelistic weekend. These groups are of enormous value in a church, and wise pastors encourage their growth.

The group and its value

How big should these groups be? Not more than a dozen or fifteen, or the evening becomes yet another presentation rather than a time of sharing, and that defeats the whole object. It should be kept small, and there needs to be some change of membership after a couple of years, or the group becomes rather stale and entrenched – so much so that it may resent new members joining.

People will ask you what the value of such a group is. After Alpha you will be well placed to give an answer. It is an opportunity to meet other Christians in a relaxed atmosphere and develop friendships. It is an opportunity for inductive Bible study, in which everyone can contribute their thoughts. It is a forum for the honest facing of doubts and questions. It is a chance to discuss and apply the Sunday sermon. It is a context in which doubts and fears, joys and hurts can be safely shared. It is a place for food, laughter and mutual support. It is a place where people matter more than structures and programmes, and where it is OK for anyone to come in and say, 'I'm feeling lousy and depressed tonight,' and be ministered to by the group, whatever damage that does to the planned programme! It is a place where prayer can be offered for personal, parish and national needs. It is a group of people who can become bonded together into God's counter-culture.

A group like this tends to get very close in a relatively short time. It will have to watch against becoming inward-looking. If the group is to remain vital, it must have an outward orientation, and needs to put on occasional evenings when non-members can be invited and hopefully join the group as a result. Above all the home group is a place where members share their lives. It is not primarily about Bible study or prayer, community service or mission. It is all about what the New Testament calls *koinonia,* 'joint participation' in Christ. This deepens the sense of community which the idea of the body of Christ suggests, and which is so greatly needed in our fragmented society. It is a place where people can come and just be, secure in the knowledge that they are accepted just as they are. 'Welcome one another,' says the apostle Paul, 'as God in Christ has welcomed you.'

Do you not think you might use your experience of Alpha to start a small group like this? It is entirely up to you whom you invite to your own home. You do not need to ask the minister's permission to go ahead with it. Indeed, in parishes where the vicar sees no need for such groups, and may give little substantial teaching in the pulpit, a group like this meeting in a home may prove to be a lifeline for hungry Christians in search of fellowship and nurture. But it is much better if the group can get going with the support of the minister, and become part of a parish plan to build lively cells of fellowship into the body of church life.

A striking example

I make no apology for having given considerable space to these house groups. They are proving an invaluable avenue for growth and expansion of Christianity all over the world. Recently in Sabah (Borneo) I spoke at a church which is made up of 220 house groups, and is growing at a tremendous pace. It has only one clergyman, but there are at least 220 leaders of these small groups, and others who act in a supervisory capacity, to help and encourage. Actually there are far more leaders than this, because every small group (wisely) has shared leadership. This of course involves the pastor in continuous and intensive training, but the payoff is tremendous. I was asked to speak at an evangelistic dinner with 400 present. I was told that half of those at the dinner would be church members, and the other 200 their friends. I was not to attempt to call for a response in any way; each guest would be personally followed up by the church member who had invited him, because all the church members had been trained in personal evangelism. No wonder the phone in the vicar's house kept going late that night and the next morning, as church members rang up to tell of some friend coming to faith through the dinner and the subsequent conversation. Needless to say there was a ready-made group for each new Christian to be drawn into – one of the 220 which constituted the church!

Just do it!

There are countless ways in which a Christian can serve the church, but the house group is paramount. Most churchpeople could not act as enablers of such a group, because they have never encountered anything like it. But you have, and you may well be one of the people who could make it fly. Why not get together with one or two others who were on the Alpha course with you, and start something? Nicky Gumbel has produced a study on Philippians called *A Life Worth Living*. Could you not begin with that? It is published, like his other books, by Kingsway. At all events, one of the great services you can offer to the Christian community is to share this small-group experience you have enjoyed in Alpha. You might like to look at the Emmaus material which is produced by a team of evangelical, Anglo-Catholic and charismatic Christian leaders and is rather similar to Alpha but covers a lot more ground. It could keep a group going for a couple of years. There is plenty of material to choose from if you get motivated. My suggestion is that you just do it!

The cursillo

The cursillo is another expression of Christianity in and through the small group. Originally coming from Roman Catholic sources in South America, it has spread through a wide variety of denominations all over the world. There is almost certain to be a national office in your country. It consists of a long weekend away together in a small group – from Thursday night to Sunday night. Generally the characteristic that people always talk about is love – they feel themselves overwhelmed by the love of God. It is quite carefully structured, with an attractive ambience and good food that has been lovingly prepared, where many nominal churchpeople find themselves face to face with Jesus for the first time in their lives. They are not the same people after that encounter, and they return to their homes and parishes on fire to pass on to others the love of God which they have received themselves. So, how about going on a cursillo, and then maybe getting involved in helping to run one?

Christian service, but not necessarily in church

One of the most common misconceptions about Christian service is that it should be done in church! Certainly in the mainline churches we have been guilty of giving the impression that to be a missionary, a pastor, a doctor or a teacher may be a vocation, a call from God, whereas being a bus driver, a politician or a factory worker is merely a job. What a scandalous denial of the incarnation, where the Lord of glory got his hands dirty in the workshop of a provincial town. What a scandalous denial of the body of Christ, where every limb is needed if the whole body is to be healthy. All Christians are called to serve the Lord with integrity in the job, the marriage, the social situation where their lot is cast. There is no division between the 'sacred vocation' and the 'secular job'. The incarnation of Jesus has broken down that artificial and utterly disastrous wall between the secular and the sacred.

So your main service to the cause of Christ may well not be in church at all. It may be in your home, in your leisure activities, or the care you lavish on others. Voluntary agencies, in hospitals, libraries, feeding the hungry, striving for justice, are extensively staffed by Christians. Indeed, if all the Christians withdrew, many of them would fall to the ground. Your main sphere of Christian service might lie there. But it might equally well be in your job, through the quality of your work and relationships, perhaps giving leadership in a trade union or on the Board. So let nobody dream of restricting Christian service to church: being a treasurer, a greeter, a sidesperson, or a choir member. It extends to the whole of life. My aim is to please Christ by doing what he would do in my professional life and my family life if he were here today.

In the USA they have sold thousands of little bracelets with the letters DWJWD inscribed upon them, to remind the wearer to 'do what Jesus would do'. That may not be your style, but the sentiment should govern every Christian's life. I want the whole of my life to speak for Christ, don't you? I believe in every member ministry within the body of Christ, and I want to live it out. Don't you? Very well, why not pray something like this:

Lord, I really want to make a difference for you – in the home, at work, at church and in my leisure time, in my ambitions, my use of money, and the way I treat other people. Please show me any particular ministry you want me to undertake, any vision you want me to initiate as a member of your body. And then give me the staying power to go for it and stay with it.

You will then be a bit like a computer that is turned on, with an empty screen, ready for him to write what he likes on it. 'Teach me your will, O Lord, and I will follow it to the end,' said the psalmist. Not a bad motto. It is the Lord's job to guide me. It is mine to obey. And we can be confident that he will indeed guide us if we are open to it. There is a whole world of need out there, and the Lord must be delighted to have members of his body who are willing to obey his directions, get stuck in and alleviate some of that need.

Talents and responsibilities

One thing more before we leave this subject of church. Never forget that we all belong. It is no good slating the church for its many failings. We are all part of it. And once we have come to a living faith we shall want the body of Christ, to which we now belong, to be as beautiful and effective as possible. So please take seriously your responsibilities. Are you gifted with young people? With the elderly? In teaching children or training leaders? Then get involved. Not for ever (this is a fear which stops many people volunteering) but for, say, a three-year term. That would be a marvellous way to serve the Lord, in the role of Sunday school teacher, youth leader, hospital visitor, PCC member. And then stand down, have a rest or do something else. Don't be blackmailed by the wail, 'There's nobody else – do stay.' There is always somebody else. Don't allow anyone to make you feel indispensable. The graveyards are full of indispensable people.

Or it may be that you should stand for office – on the church council, as a lay leader, a churchwarden or elder. So often these jobs have not changed hands for years, and effectiveness declines without the infusion of fresh blood. Get to the place where decisions are made, and use your God-given zeal to help direct the life of the church. If you are a young person, you might consider giving a year of your life as a short-term missionary assistant (the opportunities for this sort of work are enormous and there is scope for whatever skills you may have). Alternatively, you could offer yourself as a lay worker in a parish, getting food and shelter and an allowance, but finding deep fulfilment in working for others for a year before pursuing your career. There is a crying need for sacrificial service like this. As a young person you will probably have little money to contribute, but you have lots of enthusiasm and energy. What about offering that to the Lord?

The long haul

But think further ahead for a moment. Could it be that God is calling you to a longer-term involvement overseas?

Perhaps as a career missionary, or to exercise a professional role in some country where you are able to make a
significant Christian impact? Such people are in great
demand – ask any missionary society. They will show you
long lists of almost every conceivable kind of job which
the overseas church is crying out for, jobs that are often left
unfilled.

Nowadays there are far more non-white Christians in
the world than white ones. And the gospel is growing
faster than at any time in human history, especially in the
Two Thirds World. Latin America, sub-Saharan Africa,
China and South-East Asia are seeing explosive Christian
growth. But while the conversion rate is high, so is the
fallout and the spread of heretical teachings. And all
because they have so few competent teachers to train the
new Christians properly. If you have a gift of teaching, you
might be able to meet a crying need by giving up a few
years to work in one of these developing countries. For
many years doctors and nurses have heeded that call, and
the good they have done is incalculable. But opportunities
abound for secretaries, agronomists, technical personnel,
theological teachers in seminary and extension work,
public health officers, accountants, and a whole raft of
professions. It is invigorating and challenging work and
most of those who undertake it find themselves poor but
very happy. Is this something you might want prayerfully
to consider if Alpha has set your heart ablaze with the
desire to use your one life strategically for God?

Or come nearer to home. Have you thought what a difficult but rewarding job it is to be ordained? The only
source of recruitment for the ministry is from the ranks of
those who are not ordained! Do you love the Lord, love
people, possess some leadership skills and a passion to
bring others to Christ and build them up in the Christian

way? Then you should at least investigate ordination. It may well not be right for you. That will depend, at least partly, on the assessment of others. But it is something to consider at least once in your life. You may fear you are too old. Not necessarily. Most denominations have permanent deacons, non-stipendiary clergy and the like, and you can join them even in retirement. Another option is to become a lay reader, as the Anglicans call it, or a lay preacher, in Methodist terms. This gives you a recognised standing from which to preach and teach the faith. It is no good complaining about the ineffectiveness of the clergy if you are not prepared to test whether you might not be called to join them!

Being and doing

Whatever our role in church and society, one of the lessons I have been slow to learn is that *being* is more important than *doing*. I am not defined before my God by the task that I do, but by the family I belong to. And that is the family of God. What a privilege! I want that membership to shine out through my speech, my behaviour, my whole being. You and I are ambassadors for Christ. We cannot escape it. The only question is whether we will be good ambassadors or not. Will we bring credit or shame upon the heavenly government we serve? For we can be sure of this. People will judge the reality and the appeal of that heavenly government by what they see in us. 'You are the body of Christ, and individually members of it.' That is the wonderful privilege and the powerful challenge which Christian discipleship puts to us.

6

The Sacraments

There was one important area which the Alpha course and *Questions of Life* hardly touched: the sacraments. There is, however, a useful discussion, 'What does Alpha teach about the sacraments?', in Nicky Gumbel's *Telling Others*, from page 192. The omission in the course itself was understandable. Alpha is designed to cross denominational barriers, and sadly the sacraments have proved to be one of the main occasions of division in the church. This is all the more ironic since Jesus gave them to us as marks of unity. But there it is. A problem instead of a bond.

We cannot afford to skate over this important subject, since it is so sensitive in many a church. Some churches say that baptism is effective for children; others deny it. Some distinguish between a baptism in water and one in the Holy Spirit. Some people rebaptise; others will not hear of it. Some say that baptism in the Spirit always brings the gift of tongues; others reject that notion. And so we could go on. It is a very difficult area.

The Holy Communion is no less contentious. Is a Communion only valid when led by someone who stands in historic descent to the original apostles? Is it a family meal in which all Christians can share, or only those of a particular denomination? Do the bread and wine represent Jesus and his sacrifice, or do they in some way convey it? Is faith necessary, or does receiving do the trick all by itself?

There are endless divisions over these two beautiful signs of beginning and continuing our Christian lives which the Lord has left us. So let us try to cut a path through the jungle. We will start with baptism.

Baptism

Baptism is the mark of Christian belonging. It is our badge. But where did it come from, and what does it mean?

Baptism – its background

There was once a professor of Church History who began his lectures – to the amazement of his students – with Abraham! But he had a point. The God who meets us in the New Testament is the same God who for centuries had been making himself known in the Old Testament. What, then, has Abraham got to do with baptism?

You will recall the early chapters of Genesis. God makes human beings, by whatever evolutionary or other means, to be the crown of his creation, to enjoy his company 'in the garden in the cool of the day'. Human beings declined the offer, and have been going their own way ever since. This breaks God's heart, and he is prepared to take endless trouble to restore relationships. So he finds one man, Abraham, who will trust and obey him. He approaches him in sheer, utterly undeserved love (which the Bible calls grace). He wants to pour his love on Abraham and make him the father of a new humanity prepared to do God's will and enjoy his company. The trouble is, Abraham is very old and has no children. So God comes to him in a vision and promises him children as many as the stars in the sky. No wonder Abraham has his doubts. Wouldn't you? So God makes a covenant, a binding agreement, with him, almost as if he cannot be trusted. And he seals this covenant with a physical sign, which was to be circumcision. There was nothing very special about it. Many of the surrounding tribes had the custom. But God took this perfectly ordinary thing and made it a physical demonstration to Abraham of the reliability of the covenant. And Abraham accepted both the destiny and its covenant sign. He circumcised himself and his male descendant, Isaac, when in due course and against all probability he was born. It became a jealously guarded mark of being a Jew, one of the covenant people. You can read all about it in Genesis 17. God came to Abraham in grace, Abraham responded in faith, and the mark of this covenant between them was circumcision. Notice in Genesis 17 that the sign could either follow faith and obedience, as it did with Abraham, or could precede it, as it did with Isaac. The seven-day-old child was entitled to the mark of the covenant, being born of a covenant family.

That is the background. Jews knew all about a physical badge of belonging. They knew that it was a seal on the covenant between God in his gracious love and themselves in trusting obedience. That physical badge to mark the grace–faith relationship between God and us continues throughout the whole Bible.

Baptism – its origins

So, God may be a covenant-making God who gives us a badge to assure us (and show others) that we belong to his people, but where does baptism come from? It all began with John the Baptist, the forerunner of Jesus. John was the biggest news to hit Palestine for centuries. His prophetic actions stirred the country to its roots. And the heart of what he did was to baptise.

It is hard for us to understand what a shock this was. Jews were clear that 'Gentile dogs' were complete outsiders, and if they wanted to be incorporated into Judaism they had to go through a ceremonial bath to wash away their Gentile impurities. But to apply a washing like this to Jews was unthinkable! Yet that is what John did, to make it very clear that none should presume on being Abraham's children. There was one door and one only into the coming kingdom of God: repentance. No pedigree, no good deeds could render it unnecessary. It was indispensable. Nobody was too bad to be included; even the notorious sinners of the day came for baptism. Nobody was too good to need it; and that included the Pharisees and priests. This baptism demanded a repentance which led to a real change of life. It was public and unashamed. It was a pointer to the last judgement: you either underwent God's judgement on sin symbolically, through baptism in the running waters of the Jordan, or else you would have to face it for real later on.

Above all, John's baptism pointed beyond itself. He told his hearers, 'I baptize you with water; but he who is mightier than I is coming, the thong of whose sandals I am not worthy to untie; he will baptize you with the Holy Spirit and with fire. His winnowing fork is in his hand, to clear his threshing floor, and to gather the wheat into his granary, but the chaff he will burn with unquenchable fire' (Luke 3:16–17). Of course, he was pointing forward to Jesus, who would bring in God's kingdom. He would cleanse the conscience of penitent people and bring the forgiveness of sins which John's baptism pointed to (see Mark 1:4) but could not confer. And he would fulfil the hopes of the prophets like Ezekiel and Jeremiah long ago that one day the Holy Spirit would no longer be reserved for special people like prophets and kings, but would be widely available for the people of God. What an amazing first instalment of the baptism teaching of the New Testament!

The baptism of Jesus

The most famous baptism candidate John the Baptist ever had was Jesus. He had done nothing wrong in the whole of his life, so it is at first sight strange that he should go in for 'a baptism of repentance'. But think about what Jesus had come to this earth for. It was primarily to break down the massive barrier of guilt and alienation from God which our sins had erected. And so here he identified with sinners symbolically in the Jordan, because the day was coming when he would do so in awesome reality on the cross. Long after his baptism in the Jordan by John he could see his real baptism as future: 'I have a baptism to undergo, and how distressed I am until it is completed!' (Luke 12:50, NIV). His cross was to be his real baptism! In John's baptism in the River Jordan, Jesus identified with sinners so as, in due time, to bring about the forgiveness of sins to which John's baptism pointed.

Several very illuminating things happened when Jesus was baptised. First, he was assured that he was indeed the Son of God. 'This is my beloved Son,' said the voice from heaven (Matthew 3:17 and parallels). Of course he did not become the Son of God at his baptism (he was the Son of God already), but he received a powerful assurance of it.

Second, he realised that he was called to the destiny of the Servant of the Lord. The voice from heaven at his baptism did not merely say, 'You are my Son,' but continued, 'In you I am well pleased.' The first half of that statement comes from Psalm 2:7, one of David's 'royal' psalms which regarded the king of Israel as in some derived sense a 'son of God'. Here was the one who really deserved the title! But the second half came from Isaiah 42:1, a passage sketching out the destiny of the Servant of the Lord. Isaiah gives us four 'Servant songs' which combine to provide an awesome picture of the suffering, death and vindication of the Servant of the Lord. Nobody had been keen to see their lives as a fulfilment of this prophecy in the centuries since Isaiah. It was waiting for Jesus, God's Servant as well as his Son.

A third aspect of the baptism was the gift of the Holy Spirit which came so powerfully and manifestly upon him. He was going to need that empowering for his work!

And finally the baptism led immediately into the start of his ministry, complete with doubts and ghastly temptations during forty days of testing in the desert. Receiving the Holy Spirit does not deliver us from having to face hard times!

So the baptism of Jesus, while being unique, has a good deal to teach us about Christian baptism. We see the gracious offer of God's Holy Spirit. We see the assurance of sonship, though for us it is adoption into the family to which Jesus belongs by right. It points to a life of costly service. And it is the commissioning for ministry. These are all strands in Christian baptism, as they were in Jesus' own. We are plunged, at our baptism, into the baptism of Jesus and caught up in its implications.

Baptism – its meaning

At last we can begin to understand the meaning of baptism. It owes much to the Old Testament, much to the baptism of John and much to Jesus' own baptism.

The Old Testament reminds us that God makes covenants with sinners like us. They originate in his grace, and they lead to our responsive faith and obedience. He gives his people a physical mark of belonging to the covenant people. Baptism takes over from circumcision as that mark, but the covenant itself remains unchanged. It is between God's grace and our response.

The baptism of John shows us that baptism is meant to bring us in repentance to receive the forgiveness of sins. Otherwise we shall have to face the righteous judgement of God. It points forward to the cleansing and indwelling of the Holy Spirit which Jesus would make possible.

The baptism of Jesus takes us much further. It was in this dramatic act that he was anointed by the Holy Spirit. It was at his baptism that he perceived his status as Son of God and his role as Servant. It was here that he received his commission for a life of ministry. Christian baptism includes all these things, because, above all else, it unites our life with that of Jesus.

Baptism – some images

The New Testament does not spend a lot of time theorising about baptism. Instead it gives us some splendidly evocative imagery. Baptism speaks of new birth (John 3:5). It speaks to us of putting on a new suit of clothes. That is

what it means in Galatians 3:27 when it says: 'For as many
of you as were baptised into Christ have put on Christ.' It
is as if we emerge from our tattered old clothes, have a
good bath, and then put on a brand new suit of clothes.
Jesus is that new suit. And with baptism we put it on.

Again, baptism speaks to us of washing (1 Peter 3:21).
The sin which keeps us from God is washed away in this
marvellous sacrament. Not, of course, that baptism has
the power to do this by itself. But it offers us the fruit of
what Jesus did for us on the cross. The gift is held out to
us in baptism, awaiting our response.

Baptism means a lot more than washing. It is the sacrament of our justification (Romans 6:3–4); that is to say
our complete acquittal before God for everything we have
done wrong. Paul insists that we who have been baptised
into Christ have been baptised into his death, and rise
from the waters of baptism clothed in his resurrection
power and standing. The charge sheet against us has been
wiped clean. The new life beckons. This is undreamed-of
generosity on God's part, and yet it is perfectly fair,
because God in Christ has dealt with our sins and our
account has been cleared. Many evangelical Christians
tend to see baptism and justification by faith in Christ as
opposites. St Paul sees them as the outside and the inside
of the same thing! Both are done for us. Both are for the
totally undeserving. Both are unrepeatable: you can no
more be rebaptised than re-justified. And both are
eschatological; that is to say they anticipate in the here and
now God's final verdict on the day of judgement. He looks
at us and says, 'That old you has died, drowned in the
waters of baptism,' just as he looks at us and says, 'The
condemning list of all your failures has been wiped out for
ever.' Yes, baptism is the sacrament of justification by the
sheer grace of God. And it is significant that the

Reformers, way back in the sixteenth century, saw it in that light. They did not repeat the baptism they had received as infants. They entered into its benefits and claimed them personally.

Baptism – a summary

Let's try to summarise. Baptism embodies God's challenge to repentance and faith. It offers us the blessings of the covenant with God. He comes to us with utterly unmerited love, and we respond in adoring faith and obedience. Forgiveness, sonship, justification, the new birth, the Spirit, the promise of life after death – all these covenant blessings are pledged to us in baptism. Baptism, as the old Reformers used to say, 'estates' these blessings on us. It gives us the title to them. We have seen too that baptism plunges us into the death and resurrection of Jesus. Death to the old life; a new life opens up. Baptism is the gateway to revolution in our standing and in our lifestyle. And it is important to realise that baptism initiates us into the worldwide Christian church, not to some denomination or other. You are not baptised Anglican or Methodist or whatever. You are baptised into Christ. Baptism is the adoption certificate into the Christian family. It is the decisive point of no return. Many a Muslim or Jewish family will cut a convert off from family, inheritance, education and citizenship when he or she is baptised. They will probably hold a funeral service for the person concerned, and have no more to do with them. Baptism has set them apart from the old life and its relationships.

There is one more important side of baptism. It was present in Jesus' baptism, and it is present in ours. Baptism is God's commissioning for service. We put on the uniform of a Christian and we go out in active service to our Commander to draw his rebel subjects back into his allegiance. When Azariah, Bishop of Dornekal in South India, took over the leadership of his diocese there were few Christians, and they were drawn mainly from the poorest and least articulate members of society. When he relinquished office, years later, their numbers had swelled dramatically to a quarter of a million. The secret? Whenever he held an adult baptism or a confirmation he got each candidate to repeat after him: 'I am a baptised Christian. Woe to me if I do not preach the gospel.' A church with that understanding of baptism is likely to grow!

Baptism – what does it do?

It is one thing to have clear views about what baptism means, but what does it do? Sometimes people who have been baptised in infancy grow up into Christ like an opening rose. Sometimes there is no sign whatever that anything at all has happened.

As is well known, the Catholics regard baptism as effecting what it symbolises. It not only points to, but invariably brings about, the new birth, the gift of the Spirit, justification and so on. But that is hard to reconcile with the New Testament, which expressly warns us against relying on outward observances if our hearts are not turned towards God. Simon Magus is a classical case in point. Here was a man who was baptised but was clearly not a Christian. He remained 'in the gall of bitterness and in the bond of iniquity' (Acts 8:23). And Paul writes, 'They profess to know God, but they deny him by their deeds' (Titus 1:16). He draws attention to thousands of Israelites who were like that. They had the mark of the covenant upon them but had never responded to it, and they all perished in the wilderness (1 Corinthians 10:1–13). 'He is not a real Jew who is one outwardly, nor is true circumcision something external and physical. He is a Jew who is one inwardly, and real circumcision is a matter of the heart' (Romans 2:28–29). The same is true of baptism. Sadly there are millions of baptised people who display no mark whatever of God's new life within them. Neither Scripture nor experience leads us to suppose that baptism by itself is enough to bring about new life in Christ. It is important to be clear about this, because many clergy seem to operate as if it were. They give the impression that so long as people are baptised, they are OK.

Protestants have reacted strongly against this almost magical view of baptism. Many of them see it as merely symbolic. It does not *do* anything at all. Now this may make sense of the hordes of baptised unbelievers to be found everywhere, but it does not do justice to the claims of the New Testament. For instance, we read that through baptism we are saved, we are buried with Christ so as to share his risen life, we are born again, and we put on Christ (1 Peter 3:21; Romans 6:3–4; John 3:5; Galatians 3:27). Nevertheless, despite this strong instrumental language, Scripture recognises exceptions. As we have seen, Simon Magus was baptised but not saved, and the penitent thief (Luke 23:43) was saved but not baptised. How can we make sense of this tangled situation?

Baptism – title deeds

We can do so by seeing baptism as the title deeds to the kingdom of heaven. In baptism God extends them to us, but we have to sign our names on them. Or, if you prefer, you can look on it as a wedding certificate. In a marriage, after the exchange of vows, the minister declares the couple to be man and wife. That is fair enough, because he knows that the signing of the register will follow in a few minutes, and consummation later on. But if either of those conditions is missing, the couple are not married even though they have said their vows. It makes a lot of sense. No normal couple would be so foolish as not to consummate their marriage. In anticipation of that consummation they are quite properly said to be married. But if for some reason like serious illness the consummation does not take place for some time, the marriage could be null and void. What is needed then is not for them to go through the whole wedding service all over again, but to supply the missing part: consummation!

Baptism is very similar. It offers us a wedding certificate to the Lord Jesus Christ, or, if you prefer, an adoption certificate into the Father's family. So it can properly be described as effecting what it symbolises. But it does not do so automatically or unconditionally. We have to repent and believe, and we have to make room in our lives to welcome the Holy Spirit.

It seems to me that the right balance is to be found in the Thirty-Nine Articles, part of the doctrinal standard of the Anglican Church:

Baptism is not only a sign of profession and mark of difference whereby Christian men are discerned from others that are not christened, but it is also a sign of regeneration or new birth, whereby *as by an instrument* they that receive baptism *rightly* are grafted into the church: the promises of forgiveness of sins and of our adoption to be sons of God by the Holy Ghost are visibly signed and sealed. (my italics)

'*As by an instrument*' stresses the general efficacy of baptism. 'They that receive baptism *rightly*' stresses that it is far from automatic. Baptism expresses the hope of God's new life, but it is like a seed: it only germinates when it encounters the rain of repentance and the sunshine of faith.

But why on earth baptise infants?

As you will know, this is a contentious issue. That is partly because there is no decisive teaching on the subject in the New Testament. No one text will settle the matter either way, and different Christians weigh the evidence differently.

The vast majority of Christians down the ages and throughout the denominations baptise the children of believers. That does not mean they are right, but it does mean there must be some good reasons for doing so, when the children are much too young to know what is going on, let alone to respond. Here are the reasons.

First, tiny children were admitted into the church of the Old Testament. They received the sign of the covenant when they were seven days old. And of course they did not know what was going on either! But God welcomed them in on the basis of their parents' faith and obedience. Circumcision was not, in their case, a sign that they had believed, but a prayerful expectation that they would. And there is one passage in the New Testament that explicitly links baptism and circumcision in this way (Colossians

2:11–12). If children were admitted into the people of God in Old Testament times, are they to be excluded from the New Testament church? Has God grown less gracious than he used to be?

Second, the entire family was baptised when proselytes from a Gentile background came over into Judaism. The father of the family made sacrifice, the males in the family were circumcised, and everybody without exception was baptised. We know that proselyte baptism provided one of the models for baptism in the New Testament. For example, they used common language about what it achieved. The rabbis would say that a person was 'like a newborn child', 'raised from the dead', 'born anew', that 'his sins were forgiven' and so forth. Clearly, Christian baptism owes something to this precedent. Are we to assume that children were no longer acceptable when a Gentile family came over into Christianity? Normally I am suspicious of arguments from silence. But when Jesus, the fulfiller of Judaism, came to a people who for thousands of years had admitted children into the covenant relationship with God at his express command (Genesis 17), and when for some considerable time they had been baptising the whole family of Gentile converts, tiny children included, he gave not the slightest suggestion, nor did his apostles after him, that the rules had changed. I find that remarkable if the Lord did not intend us to baptise children. Don't you?

Third, there are several examples in the New Testament of whole families being baptised (Acts 11:14; 16:15; 16:33; 1 Corinthians 1:16). Were there no children in these families? It is significant that in the case of the Philippian gaoler (16:33–34 RSV) only he is said to have believed, and yet his whole household was baptised. The ancients seem to have had a sense of family solidarity which is strange to us. The head of the household would act, and that action would commit the rest of them. All through the Bible God deals with families. Of course it does not mean that every member of the family becomes a Christian. Neither theology nor experience suggests that. But it does mean that all have the right to the mark of the covenant, offered them in grace, until they make up their own minds whether to respond to the Lord, or go their own way.

Fourth, Jesus accepted and blessed little children: ' "Let the children come to me, do not hinder them; for to such belongs the kingdom of God. Truly, I say to you, whoever does not receive the kingdom of God like a child shall not enter it." And he took them in his arms and blessed them, laying his hands upon them' (Mark 10:13–16). Now that is nothing to do with baptism, but it shows the attitude of Jesus towards little people. Unlike Jewish leaders of that period, he made time for them, he valued them, he rebuked those who would keep them away, he made them a model for entering the kingdom, and he blessed them – and who can doubt they were blessed? No wonder second-century writers took this passage as an endorsement of the baptism of infants.

A fifth point which carries some weight is that the church across the world was unanimous in baptising the children of believers until the rise of the Baptist movement in the sixteenth century. Many will find it hard to believe that if the baptism of adult believers was the norm in the New Testament, it should so completely and universally have changed in the sub-apostolic period and for the next thousand years and more. Yes, I know it is an argument from silence, but it is rather an impressive one! Remember what a fuss there was when it appeared that Gentiles were entering the Christian church without keeping Jewish rules? It led to a massive Church Council (Acts 15), and the reverberations are to be found all over the New Testament. I find it utterly inconceivable that if the first Christians baptised only believers, their second-century followers could come along, change everything by baptising infants, and not a squeak about it is to be found in any of the extensive literature of the second and subsequent centuries!

Defenders of infant baptism would want to make two further points. First, that the practice stresses the objectivity of the gospel. It points to the solid achievement of Christ crucified and risen, whether or not we respond to him. It tells us that our salvation depends entirely on what God has done for us, not on our own merits. And what could be less deserving, less full of achievement than a tiny baby at the font? Martin Luther, that great Reformer who so stressed the importance of justification through faith in God's grace, used to be beset by the most terrifying doubts. At such times he did not say, 'I have believed.' He was too unsure of his faith for that. He said, 'I have been baptised' (as an infant, by the way!). Baptism stood for what God had done to make him accepted. He could stand firm on that.

The other thing the defender of infant baptism would want to say is this. In any covenant there are two sides. So it is with God's covenant with us. All agree that baptism is the seal on the covenant between God's grace and our response. But you have to administer the sign or sacrament of this agreement at some time or other. Should it be attached primarily to man's response, or to God's initiative? That is the heart of the issue. It is at this point that Baptists and those who baptise children take different roads. The paedobaptist (the person who baptises children) would want to say, 'We think it is better to keep baptism as the mark of God's prior love to us before ever we respond.' It antedates the response which it evokes, and is primarily the witness to what God has done. The Baptist prefers to retain it as primarily our response to God's generosity.

The concerns of Baptists

I have outlined the reasons why many Christians baptise infants. Here are some of the reasons why many do not. They do not think that circumcision in the Old Testament is a convincing parallel to baptism in the New, because circumcision was only applied to males, and of course baptism is for all. They think, with good reason, that anything approaching indiscriminate baptism (which most of the mainline churches practise) prostitutes the sacrament and leads to nominalism: people claim to be 'Church of England' or whatever, but in reality have no living faith. Moreover, they argue that baptism is so much more real when it comes as the climax to our repentance and faith. It is also much more evocative to go down into the waters of baptism in full immersion and bid a conclusive farewell to the old life, than to have a little water sprinkled on your head. Of course, many churches, such as my own Anglican church, baptise some candidates by full immersion, but it is the exception rather than the rule. Baptists object to the false sense of security which baptism as an infant produces when it is allied to no expression of personal faith. That false sense of security affects many people. Some are even ordained without having had any personal encounter with God. Baptists point to a number of passages in Acts where baptism is clearly linked with repentance and faith, and is administered to adults. This is not surprising, because we are dealing with first-generation Christians. Of course you go for the adults first in primary evangelism! But that does not settle the question of what was done with the children of these believers.

Baptists have other points to make. 'What good does it

do,' they may well ask, 'if you are baptised and never come to Christ?' The answer is that it does you no good. It is like carrying around a cheque for a million pounds all your life and never cashing it. It is yours in the intention of the donor, but does you not the slightest bit of good until you claim it personally.

Baptists are also critical of infant baptism because babies cannot repent and believe. True, but neither could the Old Testament children who were circumcised into the covenant relationship with God at seven days old. It is absolutely essential that the baptised do repent and believe, but hopefully that will come later. Faith sometimes precedes baptism, sometimes follows it and sometimes never follows. But of course that applies to adult candidates as well, though to a lesser extent. Liturgy by itself can never bring life.

Baptists understandably dislike the way church liturgies speak of children being regenerate, born again, inheritors of the kingdom of heaven and so forth at their baptism. They have a good point. But this, surely, is the language of hope, of faith, of promise. No liturgy can create reality!

Loving coexistence

I do not think Christians are ever going to be of one mind on this subject. We need to respect one another despite our difference of practice. Those who baptise infants must be honest enough to admit that in a great many cases there is no sign of new life, and that without repentance and faith in Christ there never will be. They must give careful instruction to families looking for baptism for their children, and ensure that there is good ground for the covenant principle being applied. There is no justification for the baptism of the children of rank unbelievers. Moreover, the link between baptism and confirmation needs to be strengthened. Baptism is the sacrament of God's initiative; confirmation is the mark of man's response. Alas, nobody had taught me that when I was confirmed. I found it a very disappointing ceremony because I had not realised it was meant to embody my personal response to Christ. At that time I had no response to make.

For their part Baptists need to be very slow to rebaptise those who have already been baptised in infancy and show clear signs of being born again. There is no excuse for the rebaptism of those who manifestly enjoy life with Christ. You can no more sensibly rebaptise than have more than one adoption certificate into a family, or wedding certificate between lovers! Baptism stresses the once-for-allness of our Christian lives; the Holy Communion stresses its ongoing nature. It is a mistake to confuse them.

To be sure, some people will want the psychological

encouragement of believer's baptism by immersion, despite having been baptised as a child. When working in a church full of students, scores of whom came to Christian faith from nothing at all, I constantly met that issue. I tried to show them that as baptised people they already had the mark of the covenant. And now they had the living faith. All they needed was the opportunity to bear public testimony to it (an important part of becoming a Christian; see Romans 10:9–10). So I would interview them about their commitment in one of the main services, and then publicly pray for the Holy Spirit to fill them for a confident life of service. In most cases this met the need. Some went and got themselves rebaptised elsewhere, but I was careful to welcome them back. Even if rebaptism is a bit like getting another driving licence when you already have one, it is no reason for breaking fellowship!

There is a great deal more that can be said on this important subject, not least the whole topic of baptism in the Holy Spirit. I have tried to give a fuller treatment in my book *Baptism* (Hodder & Stoughton). But it is time to leave the sacrament of our initiation into Christ and look somewhat more briefly at the Holy Communion, the sacrament of continuing in the Christian life.

The Holy Communion

Its various names

At the heart of Christian fellowship lies the Holy Communion, Eucharist, Mass, Lord's Supper – call it what you like. Incidentally, these names are not mutually contradictory, but complementary. Each of them is significant. Each of them calls attention to one aspect of this marvellous meal. 'Holy Communion' reminds us that we come there in order to deepen our communion or fellowship with the Lord and other members of his family: this is no solitary act. 'Eucharist' draws attention to the note of 'thanksgiving' which should permeate our worship – profound gratitude and adoration for all that the Lord achieved for us through his incarnation, death and resurrection. 'Mass' is an obscure word, but it probably means either 'meal' or the 'dismissal' of the congregation in mission. This intimate family meal is intended for believers in Christ and for no others, and Justin tells us that the non-initiated (those who were 'not yet baptised') were 'dismissed' before Holy Communion, so that may perhaps be the origin of the word. 'Lord's Supper' reminds us who is host and celebrant at this meal: Jesus himself, the one who inaugurated it at the last supper he had with his friends on earth.

Nicky Gumbel gave a couple of pages to preliminary consideration of the Communion (*Questions of Life*, pp. 228–229), and I think he lovingly borrowed some headings of mine in order to make his points! I would like to develop them for a few pages.

The Passover background

If we are going to see the significance of the Communion, it is crucial to understand that is was instituted at Passover time. Ever since the great Exodus from Egypt Jews had kept this annual reminder of their deliverance from the land of bondage where their firstborn were slain under a cruel Pharaoh. It was given to the Jews to be 'a feast to the Lord; throughout your generations you shall observe it as an ordinance for ever' (Exodus 12:14). You may recall that Moses, at God's insistence, told the people to kill a spotless lamb, paint its blood over the doorway of their house, and prepare the flesh for a meal which they were to eat in preparation for the journey out of Egypt. This Passover

meal was in a very real sense a sacrifice: 'I will execute
judgments: I am the Lord. . . . when I see the blood, I will
pass over you, and no plague shall fall upon you to destroy
you, when I smite the land of Egypt' (Exodus 12:12–13).
God's judgement was averted by the sacrifical blood of the
lambs, which he had ordered to be slain. That became the
night of nights for the Israelites. It was the night of their
deliverance from a terrible fate. The night when, in reality,
they were constituted a nation under God. They never
forgot it. Succeeding Passovers were not themselves
atoning sacrifices – they were memorials of that first
atoning sacrifice, the 'passing over' of their homes by God
Almighty when judgement turned to mercy. They kept the
festival with scrupulous care every year.

The Christian Passover

It was at Passover that Jesus met with his twelve disciples
in that upper room after they had made the proper
preparations. However, this was no ordinary Passover. No
lamb is mentioned by the Gospel-writers – perhaps this
was because they realised that Jesus, the Lamb of God,
was about to inaugurate an even greater deliverance than
the original Passover: not now from Egypt but from the
bondage and the doom of sin. The shadow was about to
give way to the reality. He was the ultimate Passover lamb,
the supreme fulfilment of that long-ago deliverance. No
wonder he told them how keen he had been to celebrate
this meal with them before his death (Luke 22:15). 'The
hour', as he called it, of cosmic deliverance was at hand,
and this meal would take them to the heart of its significance.

Imagine, then, the atmosphere when Jesus took the
unleavened Passover bread and instead of giving the
normal Passover thanksgiving – 'This is the bread of afflic-

tion which our fathers ate in the wilderness' – he came out with the astonishing words: 'This is my body, which is given for you.' What could it mean? Well, what did the words of the normal Passover liturgy mean? Not that the unleavened bread which they ate was the identical bread consumed in Egypt. It *represented* that bread to them, and as they ate it they could enter symbolically into the experience of rescue to which it referred, so much so that they used to say, 'This the Eternal did for me when I came out of Egypt.' It was living it all over again, so to speak. It was *entering into the event* which constituted them a people.

And so when Jesus uttered those never-to-be-forgotten words, he meant the disciples to see his death as deliverance from a fate far worse than Egypt. Not only did the broken bread represent to them what would happen to his body on the cross, but as they ate it, they could enter symbolically into the deliverance to which it referred. They could have fellowship with him in his death and resurrection.

No less significant is Jesus' interpretation of the wine as his blood. The blood of the original lamb when applied to the doorposts of the Israelites brought salvation. They never forgot it – red wine had to be used at Passover. The Jewish words of thanksgiving before participation in this cup of wine praised God for deliverance from Egypt, and for the covenant he had made with them. It was followed by singing Psalm 116, which speaks of 'taking the cup of salvation'. So there were profound associations as Jesus spoke of the blood, the cup and the covenant. Here was the blood which ratifies the covenant. It was his own. Naturally we must avoid literalism. Drinking blood was anathema to pious Jews. The Law expressly forbade them to do it, and they regarded the very thought with horror. No, we do not literally drink the Lord's blood at the Communion. The wine symbolises his blood poured out for our salvation so powerfully that we are able to enter into the fruits of Calvary for ourselves. But we must always remember that it is the cross which is the harsh reality to which his words at the Last Supper looked forward and every Christian Eucharist looks back.

Making the most of Holy Communion

Bearing in mind that it fulfils and replaces the great Jewish Passover, how shall we approach the Communion in order to enter as fully as we can into its meaning and blessing? Some marvellous suggestions are found in 1 Corinthians 11:17–32. The whole passage is directed to a church that was misusing the Lord's Supper, and Paul writes to correct them. How grateful we can be that he did! There are six aspects of the Communion which we would do well to dwell on as we come to it.

1. Look back. At every Communion service we should look back to what our Lord did for us on the cross.

> I received from the Lord what I also delivered to you, that the Lord Jesus on the night when he was betrayed took bread, and when he had given thanks, he broke it, and said, 'This is my body which is for you. Do this in remembrance of me.' In the same way also the cup, after supper, saying, 'This cup is the new covenant in my blood. Do this, as often as you drink it, in remembrance of me.' (vv. 23–25)

Our hearts are so often cold. They need to be warmed as we contemplate afresh the sufferings and sin-bearing of Jesus on our behalf. The Eucharist is a marvellous expression of the good news of the gospel. There, graphically portrayed before us, we see his body broken and his precious blood shed for sinners like us. How can we do other than fall at his feet in adoration and gratitude? To think that he did it for me is almost too much to take in. If the

Jews rejoiced in the marvellous deliverance from the bondage and death of Egypt, how much more we should revel in the far greater deliverance from sin's guilt and power through the victory of the cross. We enter into the very fruits of Calvary in this sacrament.

Notice how powerful the symbolism is. We are offered the body and blood of the Saviour. We come with empty hands – there is nothing we can add to it. We simply kneel and receive it into ourselves. 'Nothing in my hand I bring, simply to thy cross I cling.' It is supremely the sacrament of the gospel. So let's look back to that great deliverance, reflect on what it cost him, and be grateful.

2. *Look in*

> Whoever . . . eats the bread or drinks the cup of the Lord in an unworthy manner will be guilty of profaning the body and blood of the Lord. Let a man examine himself, and so eat of the bread and drink of the cup. For any one who eats and drinks without discerning the body eats and drinks judgment on himself. That is why many of you are weak and ill, and some have died. But if we judged ourselves truly, we should not be judged. But when we are judged by the Lord, we are chastened so that we may not be condemned along with the world. (vv. 27–32)

In the days of the Exodus, leaven (yeast) was strictly forbidden at the Passover meal (Exodus 12:15), and over the years a fascinating bit of symbolism grew up. The youngest child in the household is sent to search around the house to see if he can find any yeast. If so, it must be cleared away.

Yeast is seen very often in the Scriptures as symbolic of evil. Sin grows and spreads, as yeast does in dough. Paul is clearly thinking of this when he warns the Corinthians to search their hearts to see what needs to be confessed as they come to this holy meal. It is not something to drift into casually. It is holy ground. The Eucharist does not merely bring the saving events to mind; it is a powerful spiritual force. We know how body and mind interact – after all, people get psychosomatic illnesses. Well, the spirit and the body can interact too, and if we deliberately flout the Lord's will and come with dirty hands to this holy feast, we must look out! It may have disastrous effects not only on our spiritual lives but on our health. It may become the agent for God's judgement instead of his nourishment. But if we judge ourselves and come humbly and penitently to the Eucharist, we will not be judged alongside secular society. Instead the Lord will chasten us, discipline and purify us for his glory. We all need to look in with self-examination and repentance when we come to the Communion. That is why most Christian liturgies have either the Ten Commandments or the Two Great Commandments (love to God and other people) early on in the service. They drive us to our knees in self-examination. Repentance is essential, and it may involve restitution if we have done something to rob or disadvantage other people.

3. *Look up*. Paul has already had something to say about the Lord's Supper in a previous chapter: 'Is not the cup of thanksgiving for which we give thanks a participation in the blood of Christ? And is not the bread that we break a participation in the body of Christ?' (1 Corinthians 10:16–17, NIV). Profound stuff, and not easy to take in. But what he appears to be saying is that this meal is no mere act of remembrance. It is feeding on the living and ascended Christ. It is drawing on his strength for the battles which lie ahead in the coming week. That takes us straight back to the original Passover. If you read the account in Exodus 12 you will see that whereas the blood of the lamb was painted above the door to avert God's

judgement, the rest of the animal was made into a special meal for the family, to strengthen them for the long trek ahead. Jesus himself is the food for the Christian. He is the paschal lamb. He is the bread of heaven. He is the true vine. And in the Eucharist we 'feed on him in our hearts by faith with thanksgiving' as the *Book of Common Prayer* Communion service puts it. So let's make sure we look up to him at every Lord's Supper and ask him to strengthen us with his very being, his body and blood, for all that we shall have to face in the coming days. The Communion is battle rations for Christian warriors.

4. *Look around.* Every reference to the Communion assumes that we are a fellowship, a group. There is never any suggestion of Communion being a solitary spiritual experience. Nobody can have it on their own. 'Because there is one bread, we who are many are one body, for we all partake of the one bread' (1 Corinthians 10:17). The old Passover was a community affair. So is the Eucharist. And this verse attributes to it a remarkable power. If we come with due awareness of the people around us, we will find ourselves drawn in to ever closer fellowship with them, so that increasingly we are seen to be a colony of heaven, God's counter-culture here on earth.

Once again we are brought face to face with the mysterious power of the Eucharist. Not only is it the symbol of unity as we share in the one loaf and the one cup; it also helps to create unity. *Because* there is one loaf, we who are many constitute one body. It does something. It deepens the bonds between us. That old lady, that bluff shopkeeper, that lanky youth, that friendly bus driver – all belong together in the Lord's family. All kneel together or stand side by side to receive the bread and wine, the sacred elements of his body and blood given without distinction for one and all. There is no room for pride in the face of such self-giving love, is there? No room for keeping some chip on the shoulder! No excuse for fuelling some quarrel with another member of Christ's body. We are all on a par: fellow sinners, fellow heirs of the same kingdom and fellow guests at the same table. None of us has a right to be there. We are all graciously invited by the Lord of glory. All human distinctions fall away before him.

I remember a Christian general telling me about a private under his command. They both went to the same church, and the private gave way to enable the general to receive first. But he would not allow it. 'We are all on the same level here, lad,' he said. And we are. If that were really understood in most churches it would eradicate the small-mindedness, the feuds, the grudges that so often disfigure the Christian community.

5. *Look forward*. Spare a thought too for the future which God has in store for us. The new society to which we belong may not bring in Utopia on earth. God never said it would. But each Lord's Supper should have a touch of the future glory about it. The old Passover had a future look to it. It was a foretaste of the feast of salvation which they expected in the last days, just as much as it was a memorial of God's deliverance of the nation in the past. 'On this night they were saved, and on this night they will be saved,' said the rabbis as they reflected on Exodus 12:42. 'This same night is a night of watching kept to the Lord by all the people of Israel throughout their generations.' Indeed, so strongly was this element in the Passover emphasised that each Jewish family would leave an empty place at the feast in case Elijah, the great prophet who was expected to return at the end of history, should show up! That forward look is clear in 1 Corinthians 11:26. At each

Communion we 'proclaim the Lord's death until he comes'. The Eucharist reminds us of the marriage supper of the Lamb, as the book of Revelation picturesquely calls it, the final joyful consummation of God's plan for all his people. *'Maranatha!'* cried the earliest Christians in their native Aramaic, when they sat at the Lord's table. 'O Lord, come!' You find that cry in 1 Corinthians 16:22 as a matter of fact. It is as if they said, 'Lord, you have come into this world and lived and died for us. You have brought us into your family. We see many marks of your renewing work. But, Lord, there is a long way to go. Hasten the day when you wind up your plans for the world, and bring us all to the family table in heaven.' No escapism there, you will notice. But a foretaste of the future glory to give us a sense of perspective in our daily work.

6. *Look outwards*. It is very clear both from the Passover and from the Communion service that they are intended to equip the people of God for mission. They are not nourishment alone. Not grateful reflection alone. Not the hope of heaven alone – but food for the journey, the bread of heaven to enable us to live a Christlike life on earth. In this wonderful meal you and I are proclaiming the Lord's death until he comes. The original word used there means 'announcing'. I announce that his death has saved me. I announce that his risen life sustains me. I announce that at the end of the road he awaits me. And not me only, not the Christian family only, but all who will come to trust him. The Lord has given us the inestimable privilege of being his ambassadors to pass on that glorious gospel to others as best we can. The Eucharist has an inescapable outward thrust.

So I want to look back in gratitude, look in with repentance, look up with faith for him to feed me, look around in fellowship, look forward with keen anticipation, and look out in service. Those are some of the dimensions of this marvellous service. No wonder Jesus did not intend us to celebrate it just once a year like the Passover. The first Christians did so weekly, and we would be wise to do the same. 'As often as you eat this bread . . .' said the Saviour. Let it be often. For just as baptism is the sacrament of beginning the Christian life, so the Communion is the sacrament of its continuance. It's a good word, 'sacrament'. It originally meant the Roman soldier's oath of allegiance to his general. In these two sacraments which he instituted, baptism and the Communion, Jesus offers to take us into his service and to nourish us with himself, no less. In return he expects and richly deserves the soldier's oath of allegiance – yours and mine.

7

Christian Lifestyle

Learning from the expert

I remember some years ago being struck by a remarkable film title. It was *Start the Revolution Without Me!* The Christian life seems to me to be the exact opposite of this. You could almost summarise it as a prayer to the good Lord: 'Start the revolution within me!' That is precisely what he does when we entrust our lives to him and start off as his disciples. Discipleship simply means learning from the expert.

Let's take an analogy from cricket. If you had the opportunity of tireless personal tuition from Shane Warne, wouldn't you jump at it, if you were an aspiring spin bowler? You would listen to him, watch him, glean any tips you could from him, and try to do it like he does. That is discipleship. And that is what you and I are called to. God sets before us the expert not in spin bowling but in living as a perfect human being, and he says to us, in effect, 'There is your model. Listen to him, talk to him, model yourself on him. Try to please him in the daily art of living, and you will gradually become better and better at it.'

I heard a criticism the other day of the Alpha course and its written version, *Questions of Life*. The accusation was that the whole thing was too 'happy clappy', and that the tough cost of following Jesus was side-stepped. It was Christianity without tears. Well, I have just reread the final chapter in the book, which makes it abundantly clear that following Christ is very demanding and costly. In fact the whole chapter is a sort of exposition of Romans 12, which is all about offering our bodies as a living sacrifice, holy and pleasing to God, and not being conformed to this world, but being transformed by the renewing of our mind. Then, says the apostle, you will be able to test and approve what God's will is – his good, pleasing and perfect will. The next fourteen pages of the book draw out the implications of that costly obedience. I don't call that shallow, happy clappy Christianity. Actually, the whole aspect of lifestyle is taken much further in Nicky Gumbel's follow-up book, *Challenging Lifestyle*. It takes a realistic and highly practical look at what discipleship is going to mean in today's very secular world.

And that is the theme that I want to develop a bit further. You will have learned in your Alpha course that Christian discipleship affects the whole of life. That is what Romans 12 insists. I'm going to leave that chapter alone, because Nicky Gumbel has done an excellent job on it, but I will start my exploration of what it means to follow Jesus from a sentence he quotes from St Paul: 'Then you will be able to test and approve what God's will is' (Romans 12:2, NIV). If you forget everything else in this chapter, remember that. The way to become a great spin bowler is to test and approve what the expert bowler has to show you. I recall the cricket nets in my youth when our coach, an old England player, used to say to me, 'Do it like this, me boy. Do it like this.' Very well, the way to become a really mature and useful follower of Jesus is deliberately to set out to test and approve what his will is. And then, of course, to follow it!

Motto for life

As a matter of fact, that is what Jesus himself set out to do when he was on earth. Would it surprise you to know that he had a motto, a direction-finder for his life in the midst of all the challenges and perplexities he faced? It was this: 'I always do what is pleasing to him' (John 8:29). The 'him', of course, refers to God his heavenly Father. Jesus did not operate by a rule book or a set of commands. He set about pleasing his Father in every action of every day. That is why he can be the perfect model for the disciple. He doesn't ask us to do anything he has not done himself.

If we start out on that course, it really will be a revolution within us! Most of us reckon we are pretty decent folk. Not all our friends and relations would agree, but leave that aside! Even for the 'pretty decent' it will be a revolution to start consciously trying to please Christ. And yet that is what happens in any good business relationship, or marriage relationship for that matter. It is not so much a matter of signed contracts, as of trying to please the other person. That is what the Lord asks of us. He died for us, the apostle Paul tells us, not merely to save us from the consequences of our own folly and guilt, but so that whether we are awake or asleep we may live together with him (1 Thessalonians 5:10). He wants us to share our lives with him. He wants us to please him. 'Christ did not please himself,' says Paul with masterly understatement (Romans 15:3). The implication is obvious. We should not please ourselves either, as we did in the old days when we were 'lovers of pleasure rather than lovers of God' (2 Timothy 3:4). Our aim should be that of a good soldier: 'he wants to please his commanding officer' (2 Timothy 2:4, NIV). When in doubt about the rightness of some action we cannot just 'please ourselves.

Each of us should please his neighbour for his good, to build him up. For even Christ did not please himself' (Romans 15:2, NIV). No, indeed he did not. His ambition was to please his heavenly Father and do good to others. Was it a question of the timing of his programme? He waited until he was sure when the Father's 'hour' had come. Was it the ultimate question of the manner of his death? 'Not my will, but thine, be done' (Luke 22:42). The principle is clear. We should seek to please Christ and act as his responsible agents in society.

Ethics for amateurs

Pleasing Christ. That is really all we need to know about Christian ethics and Christian discipleship! For we are not shackled to a code of conduct. We are responsible to a person, Jesus Christ. We are motivated not by the stiff upper lip of duty, but by the deep gratitude of those who have been liberated. I want to please my Lord in every aspect of my life.

The advantages of pleasing Christ

Think of that for a moment. It is radical, because it will affect the whole of our conduct – our thought life, our money, our leisure, our relationships. There is no denying that this simple principle of discipleship will change everything.

It is also very liberating. The church has not always been very good on the matter of freedom. It has been unduly conservative about its traditions, timid in allowing people their heads, and sometimes committed to policies of reaction rather than reform. But when it has acted in this way it has done so in straight contradiction of the New Testament. There we read things like: 'It is for freedom that Christ has set us free. Stand firm, then, and do not let yourselves be burdened again by a yoke of slavery' (Galatians 5:1). In an age which is dedicated to the pursuit of freedom, Jesus offers us the key to a freedom we could never enjoy without him. A liberty to do what we ought, rather than a licence to do what we want. It is a liberation deep within us, as the Spirit who brings new life in Christ progressively sets us free from the downward pull of sin.

There's another advantage in this Christ-centred ethic. It gives great flexibility. It means we are not governed by a set of unfeeling, inflexible laws which we must keep at all costs. No, we are accountable to the most loving person in all the world, and we want to please him. How we do so may change with changing circumstances.

Of course, trying to please Christ is demanding. It requires thoughtful reflection. We can't simply open the New Testament and read the answer off the page. That is true even of the Sermon on the Mount, where, if anywhere, you might think that Jesus is laying down a new code of behaviour for members of the kingdom. Is he not legislating? Not really. To be sure, he tells us that if someone hits us on one side of the face we should turn the other cheek. But if we carry that out literally it is the fastest way to make our opponent utterly furious! Literal obedience would completely destroy the principle of non-retaliation which lies behind the particular example Jesus gave. I recall chatting once to a black South African Christian in the days of apartheid. He said that when his employer shouted, 'Boy, clean my shoes!' he did it and then asked if there was any further service he could offer. There is the principle Jesus is getting at being applied to a practical situation. But he did it not by blindly follow-ing the example in the text, but by giving careful thought as to how to relate Jesus' words to the South African situation.

A very attractive aspect of this overarching principle of pleasing Christ is that it allows for a variety of practice in different circumstances. Let nobody persuade you that there is only one possible Christian response to disputed issues. See how Paul handled diverse responses to a particularly pressing issue in his day – whether the Christians should eat food that had been sold in the meat market after having been offered to an idol in a heathen temple. Most meat was sold that way. Some Christians would not touch it at any price. Others could see no harm in it. They said, 'What's the problem? These idols don't exist. To offer meat to them therefore cannot make the least bit of difference. We have one Lord and Master. He has given us food for our good. Let's eat it and be grateful.' Here is the wise response Paul made to the problem, in a modern translation.

Don't criticise [a brother Christian] for having different ideas from yours about what is right and wrong. For instance, don't argue with him about whether or not to eat meat that has been offered to idols. . . . Those who think it is all right to eat such meat must not look down on those who won't. And if you are one of those who won't, don't find fault with those who do. For God has accepted them to be his children. They are God's servants, not yours. They are responsible to him, not to you. (Romans 14:1–4, The Living Bible)

He goes on to point out that 'the man who eats meat eats it as a gift from the Lord, and he thanks God for it. The man who refrains from eating does so out of an anxiety to please the Lord, and he too is thankful.'

What a splendid, liberal and responsible approach to an ethical issue. Splendid because it is so humane. Liberal, because it takes full account of the priceless gift of Christian freedom. And responsible because it anchors Christian behaviour in all its varied forms to pleasing Jesus Christ, the supreme pattern of the good life.

A final advantage of seeking to please Christ is that it brings such joy. God does not want to make our lives a misery but to fill them with his joy. Jesus actually offered his disciples the very same joy which he showed in his own discipleship (John 15:11; 17:13). To please him does not cramp our style, any more than it cramps the style of a BMW to drive it on petrol! Instead, it sets us free to be the people we were designed to be.

So the proper attitude for the disciple is to ask, 'What would please Christ? What would he do if he were here, in the twentieth century, in my situation?' I may get the answer wrong, but I am at least going to ask the question: 'What would he do? What action on my part would be likely to bring him credit?' It often solves my problem.

Right, if that is the principle, let's see how different New

Testament writers applied it to concrete issues like suffering, money, employment, sex, death, justice and lifestyle in general. I think we shall find some very practical examples of how this aim of pleasing Christ works out in daily life. It still does not relieve us of the responsibility of reflection and application. Things in the twentieth century are a bit different from the first century. But the principle holds good.

The new suit of clothes

Let's get the overview first, before looking at specifics. Imagine you have been out getting covered with oil under your car, or liberally coated with mud from the football pitch. The first thing you do when you get home is to have a good bath, throw the old clothes into the wash, and put on a completely new set. Isn't that right? Well, that is precisely what we should aim to do as Christians who are trying to follow Jesus. 'With regard to your former way of life,' writes the apostle Paul, 'put off your old self, which is being corrupted by its deceitful desires . . . be made new in the attitude of your minds . . . put on the new self, created to be like God in true righteousness and holiness' (Ephesians 4:22–24, NIV).

He then highlights the transformation with some excellent examples.

> Therefore each of you must put off falsehood and speak truthfully to his neighbour, for we are all members of one body. 'In your anger do not sin': Do not let the sun go down while you are still angry, and do not give the devil a foothold. He who has been stealing must steal no longer, but must work, doing something useful with his own hands, that he may have something to share with those in need. Do not let any unwholesome talk come out of your mouths, but only what is helpful for building others up according to their needs, that it may benefit those who listen. (Ephesians 4:25–29, NIV)

And if this looks a bit like a list of do's and don'ts, Paul underlines the guiding principle of pleasing the Lord once again:

> Do not grieve the Holy Spirit of God, with whom you were sealed for the day of redemption. Get rid of all bitterness, rage and anger, brawling and slander, along with every form of malice. Be kind and compassionate to one another, forgiving each other, just as in Christ God forgave you. Be imitators of God, therefore, as dearly loved children, and live a life of love, just as Christ loved us and gave himself up for us as a fragrant offering and sacrifice to God. (Ephesians 4:30–5:2, NIV)

Notice how both the motivation of not grieving the indwelling Holy Spirit and the example of the Lord Jesus are put before his readers as the centrepiece of these descriptions of character transformation. And what an attractive picture it presents!

Dying and rising

In his letter to Colosse Paul varies his imagery. It is not so much old and new clothes that provides his main illustration: it is death and life. He starts with the positive: 'Since, then, you have been raised with Christ, set your hearts on things above, where Christ is seated at the right hand of God. Set your mind on things above, not earthly things. For you died, and your life is now hidden with Christ in God' (Colossians 3:1, NIV). That's the indicative. Now comes the imperative for those who want to please their Lord:

> Put to death, therefore, whatever belongs to your earthly nature: sexual immorality, impurity, lust, evil desires and greed, which is idolatry. . . . You used to walk in these ways, in the life you once lived. But now you must rid yourselves of all such things as these: anger, rage, malice, slander and filthy language from your lips. Do not lie to each other, since you

have taken off your old self with its practices and have put on the new self. . . . Therefore, as God's chosen people, holy and dearly loved, clothe yourselves with compassion, kindness, humility, gentleness and patience. Bear with each other and forgive whatever grievances you may have against one another. Forgive as the Lord forgave you. And over all these virtues put on love, which binds them all together in perfect unity. (Colossians 3:5–14, NIV)

Notice how Paul moves from the death and life theme to the old clothes and the new. They are both expressive ways of making the same point. The old self-centred life has to give way to the new life with Christ, just as the old clothes of our unregenerate character have to give way to the new.

Farewell to all that

Peter's emphasis is similar. He urges his readers to realise that their union with Christ means they must have finished with sin. They must not live the rest of their lives for evil human desires, but rather to please God: 'For you have spent enough time in the past doing what pagans choose to do – living in debauchery, lust, drunkenness, orgies, carousing and detestable idolatry. They think it strange that you do not plunge with them into the same flood of dissipation, and they heap abuse on you' (1 Peter 4:3–4, NIV). He could not be more up to date or on target, could he? That is precisely how many unbelievers treat converts to Christ. He continues:

Above all, love each other deeply, because love covers a multitude of sins. Offer hospitality to one another without grumbling. Each one should use whatever gift he has received to serve others, faithfully administering God's grace in its various forms. If anyone speaks, he should do it as one speaking the very words of God. If anyone serves, he should do it with the strength God provides, so that in all things God may be praised through Jesus Christ. To him be the glory and the power for ever and ever. Amen. (1 Peter 4:8–11, NIV)

That is the theory, so to speak. Now let's see how it might work out in specific areas of life.

Renewed minds

Our minds

Paul insists that these need a complete spring-clean. They need to be made new all over again. This does not mean we need to throw away our brains, as some Christians foolishly suggest. It does not mean that we have to start the learning process all over again. But what it does mean is that because we have come to newness of life in Christ we begin to view everything differently. The same old things, but an entirely new way of looking at them. It is as if we had poor eyesight, almost blind in one eye and short-sighted in the other, and Christ comes up to us and offers us a pair of glasses which changes all that completely. We regain 20/20 vision. And we see everything in a new light, because our perception is now channelled through those glasses. 'We have the mind of Christ,' says the apostle, with infinite daring (1 Corinthians 2:16). So we look at our finances, our investments, our job, our home and relationships, our politics, our attitude to race and justice – everything through the eyes of Christ. It is going to take time to become adjusted to this new way of looking at things – it won't come all at once – but it is all part of the transformation God wants to make in our lives.

It is really crucial for Christians to think through the implications of their faith, and not keep it in a little box labelled 'Private: religion'. We are among the comparatively few people in this post-modern age who believe in truth – objective, realistic truth which stands fast whether folk believe it or not. So we are going to have to think hard if we are to relate effectively to the relativists all around us. How are we going to persuade them that their way of looking at things simply won't hold water? We are surrounded by pluralists, people who think it does not matter what you believe so long as you are sincere, and casually reckon that all religions are equally valid and lead to God. It is no good simply shouting the gospel louder. We have to engage with the thought forms of our contemporaries and out-think them.

That is what the first Christians did. They out-lived, out-loved and out-thought the pagans. And the gospel spread everywhere. It was intellectually cogent and spiritually powerful. So it is sad when we see a mindless Christianity, which takes refuge in cosy platitudes and does not venture out into the cold winds of contemporary unbelief to argue with it and lovingly persuade it to change course. In reacting against the rationalism that has been the prevailing worldview in the West for the last 250 years, there is a danger of lapsing into a modern, unthinking, feelings-based sort of Christianity. Beware. A faith like that will not last. God has given us a mind. We are intended to set it to work on his revelation and try to apply it to our situation and our world. You know the value of books such as Nicky Gumbel's which have combined an ease of style with a depth of content. Here is someone using his mind for the gospel. We are not all as gifted as he, but we are all called to use our mind for Christ, to wrestle with problems, to break down our prejudices, and to reform our opinions when they are wrong or are based not on Christ's way of doing things but the world's. More thinking Christians are needed! What a difference it would make in the university, in parliament, in the tool shop if Christians, instead of hiding their light away, brought it to bear on the challenges and the problems of daily life. For one thing it would gain a lot of respect. For another it would change the climate in the work place. And it would certainly change our own attitude to some of the issues which follow. I shall select examples from money, sex, work, suffering and death.

Money

When a society loses almost all its values, money becomes of surpassing importance. That is what has happened to the Western world, and it is in striking contrast to the generosity, laughter and time people have for one another which you experience in Africa. There, so many people have almost nothing, but are happy and generous with it.

We have not done a good job with money in our consumerist Western world, where shopping is our major leisure occupation. Wealth has increased at a great rate, but relationships have declined as fast. We need to remember the fabulously rich King Midas who loved gold so much that finally he got his wish. Everything he touched turned to gold. Then he touched his daughter! Our late twentieth century is rather like that. We seem to have everything to live with, but nothing to live for. What difference is being a Christian going to make in this highly sensitive area?

The Bible is clear that there is nothing wrong with money, but there is everything wrong with the love of money. It breeds many evils. Greed, oppression, avarice, dishonesty, fraud, robbery, and often murder as well, all spring from the love of money. It's sad really, because money does not satisfy. Aristotle Onassis, the world's richest man, laconically observed, 'Money does not make you happy.' And long before him the Romans had recognised that money is like sea-water: the more you drink, the thirstier you get.

What is more, money does not last. Jesus spoke of the moth and rust which spoil our possessions. Today it is income tax, inflation, robberies and the vagaries of the stock market. And even if our fortune survives, it will end abruptly at death. The story is told of an American multi-millionaire who elected to be buried sitting behind the wheel of his gold-plated Cadillac. The gravediggers had to use a bulldozer to excavate the grave, and as the car with its dead occupant was being lowered into it by a crane, one of the workers turned to the other and said, 'Man, what a way to live!' Far from it. However much we make, we leave it all behind. So how shall we use money constructively as Christians?

Advice from the New Testament

The New Testament gives us several pieces of sound advice. First, we are not meant to trust in our money. We must resist the temptation to make it our security. Paul warns those who are rich in this world not to be arrogant (an attitude which often accompanies great wealth) nor to 'set their hopes on uncertain riches but on God who richly furnishes us with everything to enjoy' (1 Timothy 6:17). One of the insidious dangers of wealth is that it tends to make us independent of God. If we have a big bank balance why bother to trust him? And you don't have to be rich to trust in money. Poor people, too, often feel that if only they won the lottery all would be well. It would not. Only today I read of a woman who won £1.2 million on the lottery and within a year was in prison after knowingly accepting half a million in stolen bank funds. Rich and poor Christians alike must remember that we have one security only: God himself. In poverty and wealth I am his and he is mine, and that is enough. 'Keep your life free from the love of money,' writes the author of the letter to the Hebrews. 'Be content with what you have; for he has said, "I will never fail you nor forsake you." Hence we can confidently say, "The Lord is my helper, I will not be afraid; what can man do to me?"' (13:5–6). One Christian friend of mine, himself very poor, once had his few choice possessions stolen from a friend's locked car. 'No matter,' he wrote. 'They are welcome to my stuff. But praise God, they can't take Jesus from me.' I have an architect cousin who has remained poor, largely because he refused to go after bad debts. But his joy and liberation as a Christian light up all who know him. If Christians as a whole were less attached to their possessions and more ready to trust God over money, it would make a big impact on society.

Second, the Bible is insistent that we should learn to give substantial amounts of our money away. In the Old Testament it was 10 per cent plus special gifts at different points in the year. In the New Testament there is no precise amount laid down, but it can hardly be less than that if we love Jesus, can it? Do you remember what happened when Jesus came to the home of that tax crook, Zacchaeus? He was so magnetised by the love of Jesus that he said, 'Behold, Lord, the half of my goods I give to the poor; and if I have defrauded any one of anything, I restore it four-fold' (Luke 19:8). Jesus' comment was instructive: 'This shows that salvation has come to this home today.' Zacchaeus' giving was the yardstick of the reality of his conversion. I read recently of a Christian who had a terrible nightmare. He dreamed that he had to live on only ten times as much as he put in the church collection!

I cannot resist telling the story of when I was speaking at a conference in Jerusalem some years ago. One lady's suitcase was lost in transit. In it she had packed a good deal of Christian literature in Hebrew and Arabic for free distribution in Jerusalem. Efforts to trace it failed, until the very last day. The bag turned up, damaged, but with its contents intact. Inside there was a note which read: 'I stole this from you because I was a thief, but after reading your cards I decided that your way, the way of the Lord, was the only way. So I am returning this to you and am returning to the ways of the Lord. You have saved my soul, and I am now high on his way. Bless you.' Greed had been replaced by God in his heart. The mark of new life was a theft restored. It spoke volumes about the inner change in that man. That is what Paul had in mind when he wrote to new converts in Ephesus: 'Let the thief no longer steal, but rather let him labour, doing honest work with his hands, so that he may be able to give to those in need' (Ephesians 4:28). It's a radically new attitude to money. And it is Jesus who brings it about.

A third characteristic of the financial life where Christ has been given control is generous giving. Paul could write of the Macedonian Christians:

> Out of the most severe trial, their overflowing joy and their extreme poverty welled up in rich generosity. For I testify that they gave as much as they were able, and even beyond their ability. Entirely on their own, they urgently pleaded with us for the privilege of sharing in this service to the saints. And they did not do as we expected, but they gave themselves first to the Lord. (2 Corinthians 8:2–5, NIV)

Generous giving despite extreme poverty. Regarding giving as a privilege rather than a hassle. And the whole thing springing from deep dedication to the Lord. That is Christian giving. It is different from anything else on earth.

Of course, that is only the start of the financial revolution. It will mean generous contribution to aid programmes when urgent need arises. Christians are generally among the first to supply aid when disaster strikes. Naturally, for 'if anyone has the world's goods and sees his brother in need, yet closes his heart against him, how does God's love abide in him?' (1 John 3:17). The New Testament writers are not at all embarrassed to talk about money. They tell us, for instance, not to judge others by their clothes or their money, and not to dress extravagantly and eat luxuriously when others are in need. They tell us that we have a responsibility to be scrupulously fair and generous towards any people we may employ, remembering that we have an Employer in heaven. They tell us we can invest our money in lives, by contributing to the cause of the gospel throughout the world. They remind us that not only the proportion of our income which we give direct to God belongs to him – so does the rest. And we are accountable to him for how we spend it. Do you see how the Lord refuses to be boxed away in some little religious compartment of our lives? He wants to permeate the whole of life.

Sex

If money is one of the areas in which a Christian attitude is very distinctive, sex is another. No topic is more thought about, flaunted, discussed and regarded as a matter of personal choice. The 1960s brought about a sexual revolution which is still escalating. How are we to treat this most powerful of all our urges?

The example of Jesus

What would Jesus do? What *did* he do, for that matter? He seemed to have his sexuality under complete control. He mixed with equal ease among men, women and children.

His loving care reached out to both sexes with equal generosity. There is no suggestion anywhere in the records that have come down to us, Christian or non-Christian, that he behaved with any suspicion of impropriety or ever uttered a smutty word. Did that make him an inhibited puritan? Not at all. He lived life to the full. He was utterly balanced. He was suffused with a happiness which communicated to all he met. Yet he elected to remain a bachelor. He clearly was not influenced by the 60s morality!

Only two views on sex

There are basically two views you can take about sex. One is to see it as a toy, a plaything, which you are entitled to indulge as and when you can – and some would add 'so long as it does not hurt anyone'. The other view is to see sex as sacramental – the outward embodiment of total commitment between two people. Intercourse both expresses that commitment and enhances it.

Jesus opted wholeheartedly for the latter view. He saw sex as the sign and seal of a one-man-and-one-woman relationship which was both permanent and exclusive of all others. And he derived that view not from some arcane rule book but from God's original purpose in creating human beings. He saw man and woman as equal in value but different in function within the partnership. And he saw their marriage as the nearest we can get on earth to understanding what God is like. God is no far-off despot, ruling the world like an arbitrary tyrant. He is a trinity of love and self-giving, complementary persons within an indissoluble unity. And he has made human beings capable, in marriage, of getting somewhere near that. In this sense, among others, we are made in the image of God. Wow!

And when questioned about the propriety of divorce

Jesus did not wax judgemental about it, but pointed people back to the original purpose of marriage. It was the closest of all relationships, 'bone of my bones and flesh of my flesh', and for that reason 'a man leaves his father and his mother and cleaves to his wife, and they become one flesh', and they 'were both naked, and were not ashamed' (Genesis 2:23–25). You can detect here no homophobia, no tirade against adultery and fornication. No, he set out the ideal, and he lived that way. One man, one woman for keeps – or singleness. Those are the options according to Jesus. And if you wonder why he adopts this tough line, the answer is plain. It is because love, marriage and sex are meant to go together by the God who invented all three.

Intercourse is the closest possible relationship we can have with another human being, and God's intention is that we use it as a profound symbol of the inner love we have for that other person; a love that, like God's own love (of which it is a reflection), is fully personal, does not act selfishly and does not give up. What passes for love in the casual liaisons of our day is often depersonalised, as in pornography, which concentrates not on the person but on the genitals. It is often selfish, as in the attitude 'What kicks can I get out this?' And it is generally short-lived, leaving behind a lot of disillusionment, hurt and loneliness as the erstwhile partner is discarded on the human scrap heap. I heard in a television programme on divorce the other night a tearful teenager say, 'It's weird that the parents who made me can't now even talk to one another.' That is what happens when the Maker's instructions for sex and marriage are rubbished.

Infidelity

Infidelity brings acute pain and bitterness. It usually carries a lot of guilt. It has to be covered up by lies and hypocrisy. It dehumanises sex into an act in itself, not the summit and the bond of a lasting relationship. It traumatises the partner who is jettisoned, and hardens the one who has initiated the break. It artificially separates sex from love, fidelity, companionship and children. It betrays an inability to control our instinctive drives. It undermines trust. The man who cannot be trusted to master himself before marriage cannot be trusted to do so in marriage. Inevitably the woman he ends up marrying (who, hypocritically, he would like to be a virgin!) will have to live with the gnawing doubt, 'Will he remain faithful to me when my back is turned?' And what sort of a foundation for marriage is that?

It is interesting that even Masters and Johnson, the celebrated American sexologists, have come to the conclusion, after endorsing the permissive lifestyle for decades, that the only permanently satisfying sexual relationships are those between partners who are exclusively faithful to one another. And they are certainly not guided by any Christian conviction – merely by noticing from extensive observation what happens when people engage in multiple partnerships.

Basic attitude

So our basic attitude to sex is not difficult to untangle if we really set out to please Christ. It is not surprising that the New Testament writers are clear that conversion to Christ makes a massive difference in this particular area of our lives. Take, for example, the Corinthians, who lived in the Vanity Fair of the ancient world. Here is the change the apostle Paul noticed in them: 'Do not be deceived; neither the immoral, nor idolaters, nor adulterers nor homosexuals, nor thieves, nor the greedy, nor drunkards, nor revilers, nor robbers will inherit the kingdom of God.

And such were some of you. But you were washed, you were sanctified, you were justified in the name of the Lord Jesus and in the Spirit of our God' (1 Corinthians 6:9–11). A fascinating passage. For one thing it sets a very clear Christian standard before us. For another, it does not single out sexual sins for special treatment, but puts them alongside furious language, robbery and idolatry. But most amazing of all is the way the apostle can be confident that they have said goodbye to all that. It is part of the old suit of clothes they threw away when they came to Christ.

Reflect on his words to the Ephesians which we glanced at earlier:

> Walk in love, as Christ loved us and gave himself up for us, a fragrant offering and sacrifice to God. But immorality and all impurity or covetousness must not even be named among you, as is fitting among saints. Let there be no filthiness, nor silly talk, nor levity, which are not fitting; but instead let there be thanksgiving. Be sure of this, that no immoral or impure man, or one who is covetous (that is, an idolater), has any inheritance in the kingdom of Christ and of God. Let no one deceive you with empty words, for it is because of these things that the wrath of God comes upon the sons of disobedience. (Ephesians 5:2–6)

Impurity, filthy language, dirty jokes – they are not fitting among Christians.

Again, as we saw in Peter's first letter, he encourages his readers no longer to be guided by human passions but by what is pleasing to the Lord, and continues, 'Let the time that is past suffice for doing what the Gentiles like to do, living in licentiousness, passions, drunkenness, revels, carousing, and lawless idolatry' (1 Peter 4:3). The writer to the Hebrews puts it with great economy of words: 'Let marriage be held in honour among all, and let the marriage bed be undefiled; for God will judge the immoral and adulterous' (Hebrews 13:4).

Two important considerations

Two things are important to stress before we leave this intensely personal and complicated subject. The Christian attitude to sex and marriage, which we find consistently throughout the New Testament, is not a new legalism. It is not because Christians are against sex that they are hot on chastity before marriage and fidelity within it. On the contrary, it is because we value it so highly. Sex is too good a gift of God to cheapen. It is no mere animal coupling, but the deepest way in which two people can share each other's lives and express mutual self-giving. It is fun. It is exhilarating. It is satisfying. But take it away from the context of marriage and it becomes dishonest, for it isolates sexual unity from all the other areas of self-commitment which are meant to go with it. It is acting a lie. And Christians are not children of the lie, but of the Lord. They do not want to keep a rule book; they want to please their Lord. That is what keeps them on the straight and narrow. Paul encourages his readers to live their whole lives 'in order to please God'. He is confident that they are doing that, and he urges them to do so more and more. He reminds them that the Lord they want to please looks for their sanctification, their cleaning up – 'that you abstain from immorality; that each one of you know how to control your body [which could possibly be translated 'take a wife for himself'] in holiness and honour, not in pagan passion'. He continues, 'for God has not called us for uncleanness, but in holiness. Therefore whoever disregards this, disregards not man but God, who gives his Holy Spirit to you' (1 Thessalonians 4:1–8).

The trouble is that we are incapable of living this holy life on our own. We simply are not strong enough. And God knows it. That is why he has given us his Holy Spirit. Paul ended the quotation above on precisely this note. A holy God requires holiness in his people. He knows they are not by nature holy, and so in his generosity he gives them his Holy Spirit. That Holy Spirit lives within us once we have become Christians. And part of his work is to produce Christlikeness of character in us. We shall be looking more closely at the work of the Spirit in the next chapter. But for now, the good news is that he is immensely powerful. He lives within us. And so we are able to break habits that otherwise would be too strong for us – if we call on him for his help.

So there you have it in a nutshell. Do you want your Christianity to affect your sex life? First, examine the attitude and example of Jesus. Second, seek to please him in what you do and what you allow yourself. Third, rely on his Holy Spirit to enable you to approximate to that goal. And when you make a mess of things, come back at once for his cleansing and recommissioning.

Now let's look at another area of life which gets transformed by the fundamental Christian ethic of seeking to please Christ in everything.

Work

We spend most of our lives at work, and it is important to be clear that our Christian work is not something that we do for the church in our all-too-limited spare time. It is something we do for Christ all day long in our work time. It is not a matter of church jobs done, but of Christian attitudes adopted. And it shows most sharply and most convincingly in our daily work.

Employees

Are you an employee? Then at work you will want to do your job not just to get by, to collect your pay packet, or to keep on the right side of the boss. You are working for Jesus, and you will want to turn out work of which he could be proud. Can you imagine any shoddy workmanship coming from his carpentry shop in Nazareth?

> You employees, put your backs into the job you do for your earthly employers, not only trying to please them when they are watching you, but all the time. Do it willingly because of your love for the Lord and your desire to please him. Work hard and cheerfully in all you do, as people who are working for the Lord and not merely for the bosses, remembering that it is the Lord Christ who is going to pay you, giving you abundant wages from all that he owns. (Colossians 3:22–24, my translation)

I once came across a Chinese pastor who had been ejected from his church and subjected to the 'purge' of Mao's Cultural Revolution. He was made to labour for years on a soul-destroying assembly line in a factory. He aimed to carry out what Paul had written, and do even that mean job for Christ. Years later, when he and his colleagues had been released, he was surprised to find many of them crowding into his church and becoming Christians. He wanted to know why. 'Oh, it was your cheerfulness in that dismal job that struck us,' they said. 'You clearly had something we lacked, and we want it for ourselves!'

Employers

Are you an employer? Then your attitude to your workers will not be to see how much profit you can make out of them and how cheaply you can achieve wage settlements. No, you bosses must be scrupulously just and fair to all your employees. Always remember that you too have an Employer in heaven (see Colossians 4:1). James is even more forthright in his letter. He slates rich employers who have grown fat by fleecing their workers. He tells them that their gold and silver are corroded, and their rich clothes are rotting. They have hoarded their wealth, but they will have to face God at the end of the day: 'Look! The wages you failed to pay the workmen who mowed your fields are crying out against you. The cries of the harvesters have reached the ears of the Lord Almighty. You have lived on earth in luxury and self-indulgence. You have fattened yourselves in the day of slaughter' (James 5:1–5, NIV). James has a passionate social conscience. He is clear that 'faith without works is dead' (2:26).

When there are Christian people on both sides of industry who look beyond their immediate employment to the Lord and what he would want, then you begin to find a new harmony coming into the firm. But when the God factor is left out, there is a tendency for rival policies of greed to govern business and industry, and that is good neither for the company nor the country.

In the workplace

David Prior is a friend and erstwhile colleague. For many years he had a fruitful parish ministry by working, in the heart of London, on how Christianity can best be implemented in the market-place. At a conference recently where we were both speaking he came up with some extraordinarily illuminating insights on the subject of the Christian and work, broadly based on Ephesians 2:7–10. He pointed to the universal human experience of exquisite moments, the eternal longings and the endless questions which mark our humanity, and yet find no fulfilment in our daily work. They are pointers to God, and the answers are to be found in God alone. But he saw in the Ephesians passage five perspectives on our daily work which are very suggestive.

First, its *limitations*. We are not 'saved' (in the sense of finding our complete fulfilment) by 'works', however good they may be in themselves. Our fulfilment and our meaning cannot be exhaustively defined by the jobs we do.

Second, our *identity*. We are God's 'workmanship', literally his *poem* (2:10). What we are is more important than what we do, though we often assume otherwise. We are not human doings but human beings!

Third, our *resources* (2:10). Once we are 'created in Christ Jesus' a whole new set of resources opens up. We need to tap into those resources. David told us of a business man who was involved in a very strained and contentious Board meeting. The point at issue was not one on which he had any particular expertise, but as he sat praying and reflecting, God seemed to give him an insight, which he then shared with the Board. It proved decisive in settling the matter. The chairman, amazed, asked him how he had come up with his contribution. He replied that he had been praying. 'Then I am very interested,' said the chairman. Such unexpected resources would be very useful for business! God gave him wisdom. It is part of his 'riches in glory in Christ Jesus' on which we are invited to draw.

Fourth, David drew attention to *purpose*. God has prepared good (literally 'beautiful') works for us to do (2:10). Quality work. That is what we are called to. The word suggests both ethics and attractiveness. To apologise to an inferior, to admit one has made a mistake – these things are simply not done in many a firm, but when a Christian does them in order to please Christ, it is the right thing, it gets noticed and it often sparks changes in other people.

Finally, *lifestyle*. David pointed out that Christ's way or 'walk' stands out in sharp contrast to the 'following' life-style, the way of the crowd, which is thoughtlessly adopted by so many at work. The believer is, if necessary, prepared to stand up and be counted. But it will cut no ice unless his life is impressive. I recall one fascinating example he gave of a young woman lawyer, of whom this was true. In her Articles she had worked with a Christian company. She was then hired by a firm of corporate lawyers, who had no Christian values at all. Vast and totally unreasonable demands were made on all the staff. Morale collapsed, and the atmosphere in the office was tense. The boss was a workaholic who expected everyone else to be the same. So she went and confronted him in his office and said to him, 'You are ruining this practice.' A very bold thing to do for a Christian woman of twenty-six in her first job! The boss was visibly shaken, but to everyone's amazement he embarked on a course of radical change, and before long the atmosphere in that firm was entirely different and the output far more humane (and no less effective!). The message is plain. At work we need to be actively seeking to please Christ, and that will ensure a quality of life which will win us a hearing if and when a stand has to be made.

Suffering and death

One could go on for a long time looking at different aspects of our lives that get revolutionised once we set about seeking to please Christ. But perhaps one more will suffice. The rest we can work out on our own, for 'we have the mind of Christ' (1 Corinthians 2:16).

Let us then take a cool look at suffering and death. We dread them, but we all have to face them. Does being a Christian make any difference to us as we have to face these awesome realities?

This is not the place to discuss the philosophical problem of evil and suffering. Tomes have been written on the topic, and nobody has solved it completely. The Bible never gives us an exhaustive explanation about the presence of evil, pain and death in our world. But it provides some solid clues. It gives us enough light to live by, and indeed to die by.

Why all the pain?

This is a profound mystery, and Nicky Gumbel has addressed it head-on in the first chapter of his *Searching Issues*, the discussion guide to the Alpha course. Now is not the time to examine it in depth, since there are many thoughtful books on the subject, but here are some brief reflections.

The nature of our world has something to do with it. If there is to be any consistency at all in the world (and there would be no life without it) then the knife that cuts wood must also be able to cut your throat, and the fire that warms your chilled hands can also burn you if you get too close to it.

Moreover, a great deal of the suffering and pain in the world is caused by human wickedness or laziness in one form or another. Think of lung cancer and smoking. Think of plane crashes and the careless mistakes of mechanics, radar operators or pilots. Think of wars and the pride and ambition which generally start them. Most suffering is due to human frailty, human sin. And God cannot overrule that without taking away our freedom, the very thing that stamps us with his image and distinguishes us from robots.

Then the Bible is very clear that the existence of Satan has a lot to do with the pain and evil in this world. This supreme anti-God force seeks to ruin everything good that

God has made. The devil is out to spoil personal life by sin, family life by discord, national life by war, and physical life by disease.

What is more, we all belong together. Nobody is an island. What we do affects others. If one limb in the body of humanity is hurting, the whole is affected, just as it is in our human bodies. And that has a great deal to do with suffering. Think of the AIDS victims who are born HIV-positive because of their parents; the alcoholics who inherited the tendency from drunken parents; the victims of disasters where thousands have died because of inadequate international efforts to reach them. We are interdependent, we human beings and our environment. Mankind's rebellion against God has affected not just ourselves but our habitat, as we are belatedly discovering. We are not mere individuals. We are part of a common humanity. And it is a tainted stock.

When you come to think about it, the sheer randomness with which suffering strikes is not so surprising after all. It is rather like chickenpox. Once the virus is in your bloodstream the actual spots occur at random. There is no rhyme or reason in where they turn up. It is like that with suffering in the body of humanity. It does strike at random. It is no good asking, 'Why should this happen to me?' any more than we ask with chickenpox, 'Why should this spot occur here?' In both instances the disease has to be met, and cured, at its root. Suffering as a whole is linked in some mysterious way with sin as a whole, though individual suffering is not by any means necessarily related to individual sin. The cure must be radical.

What has God done about it?

Everyone has to face suffering and eventually death, but God has done something very significant about it. The cross of Jesus is, of course, what he has done. And from that cross four beams of light shine out on our problem.

First, the cross shows that *God is no stranger to pain*. He is the suffering God, and you can look in vain for any parallel in any other faith. Whatever the ultimate causes of suffering, God has got himself involved. In World War Two the SS hanged three Jewish lads in Auschwitz. Two died quickly, but one of them took nearly half an hour to die. The other prisoners were forced to watch. Eli Wiesel, prophet of the Holocaust, cried out, 'Where is God now?' and a Christian, who was imprisoned there too, heard as it were a voice within him saying, 'He is there. He is hanging on that terrible gallows.' Yes, the cross shows that God knows all about suffering, and he continues to suffer in and with all the sufferings of humanity. Ever since Bethlehem he has remained one of us. He did not give us an answer to the problem of pain – he shared it. He did not explain it – he accepted it.

Second, the cross shows that *God loves on through pain*. If you are ever tempted to feel, in your sufferings, that God has betrayed you and no longer cares, think of Jesus on the cross. He was never closer to his Father's heart than when he was hanging there. God loved him through it all. God the Father trusted him to achieve salvation for the whole world. Despite the awful sense of isolation and darkness which Jesus underwent as he bore away the sins of the whole world, he was able to come through it and commit his soul to his heavenly Father as he died. We can do the same. Our dark night of the soul will never be as black as his was. We are not left desolate and unloved when we suffer. We may not understand what we are going through, but the cross of Jesus assures us that suffering need not cut us off from the love of God.

Third, the cross shows how *God uses suffering and*

pain. God does not design suffering for any of his creatures, but he uses it, evil though it is. He makes good come from the evil. The cross was unspeakably evil, and yet God has brought untold blessing to millions through it. God does the same in nature. Think of the way an oyster uses the irritation of grit to turn it into a pearl. God does it in human character. Think of qualities like courage, self-sacrifice and endurance which spring only from the soil of suffering. And he does it in our spiritual lives too. He may use pain to reach us. I have known people turn to God when brought up short by some terrible accident or bereavement. He may use it to teach us some lesson we are reluctant to learn. He may use it to equip us for usefulness in his service. Remember Paul had a 'thorn in the flesh', whatever that was, and although God did not take it away in answer to the apostle's prayers, he did pour his wonderful strength into Paul's weakness. 'He said to me, "My grace is sufficient for you, for my power is made perfect in weakness." Therefore I will boast all the more gladly about my weaknesses, so that Christ's power may rest on me. That is why, for Christ's sake, I delight in weaknesses, in insults, in hardships, in persecutions, in difficulties. For when I am weak, then I am strong' (2 Corinthians 12:9–10, NIV). God can use our suffering in that same positive way, if we allow him to do so.

Fourth, think of what the cross led to: the resurrection. You can never separate them. In the cross we see *God's triumph over pain and death*. It is the first instalment of his new life for us individually and for our world. In John's account of the cross a prominent theme is Christ reigning from the tree. He looked the ultimate loser, but he was the ultimate winner. We have seen that pain as a whole is occasioned largely by sin as a whole. On the cross Jesus dealt with both at their root. He fought Satan and won. He took sin's curse upon himself and drew its fangs. He drained the cup of suffering and won through to Easter Day.

The great painter and sculptor Michelangelo once broke out in indignant protest against his fellow artists, who were for ever depicting Christ dead on the cross. 'Paint him instead as Lord of life. Paint him with his kingly feet planted on the stone which held him in the tomb.' What an important point – even if Michelangelo did not keep to it in his own artistic work! We will never begin to understand suffering if we restrict it to the small time frame of this life. It is part of our preparation for eternity. Christ died and rose again. And those who belong to him will share not only in his pains but in his victory. The whole of Christian optimism and hope is based on the resurrection of Jesus Christ from the dead.

Implications

This has a number of vital implications. If we understand them and live them out it will set us apart from what Paul calls 'others who have no hope'.

It means that death is not the worst thing that can befall us. It is horrible. It is an enemy. But it is an enemy Christ has beaten. And he will hold our hand as we go through the cold waters of death's river. He knows the way. He will bring us safe with him to the other side. The end of the road is not a casket rotting in the ground. It is being with the risen Christ for ever in the glory of his Father's home. John has a marvellous picture of heaven as a new creation, and the church as Christ's bride entering into it:

> And I heard a loud voice from the throne saying, 'Now the dwelling of God is with men, and he will live with them. They will be his people and God himself will be with them and be their God. He will wipe every tear from their eyes. There will be no more death or mourning or crying or pain, for the old

order of things has passed away.' He who was seated on the throne said, 'I am making everything new!' Then he said, 'Write this down, for these words are trustworthy and true.' (Revelation 21:3–5, NIV)

The solid ground of Easter should make an enormous difference to us as we contemplate the inevitable pain and death that await us.

It means that we need never fear we shall be left to face it alone. He has promised that he will never fail us nor forsake us, and so we need not be afraid (Hebrews 13:5). What a comfort it is to have him with us in the dark hours of suffering!

It means that we can catch a glimpse through the door of death into the beautiful garden of heaven. The door may look fast locked, but it has opened to his touch.

It means that we have no reason to be inconsolable when a loved one dies in the faith of Christ. Naturally we shall mourn and go through the various stages of that painful process. But we shall not 'grieve as others do who have no hope' (1 Thessalonians 4:13).

It means that we can see all disasters, and our own inevitable death, in the light of Easter, and can face them with some peace when our turn comes.

Truly Jesus brings transformation into every aspect of the Christian's lifestyle!

8

The Meal and the Spirit

Leaving out the difficult stuff

Among the most significant chapters in *Questions of Life* are the three about the Holy Spirit. And during the Alpha course, it is the weekend or day away on the person and work of the Holy Spirit that many churches decide to skip. Interesting, isn't it? We try to get around the hard bits. The meal? That's a lot of work. Let's have a cup of tea instead. The Holy Spirit stuff? That's a bit extreme. Let's cut it out. And guess what? The churches which do that often come up with a complaint: 'Well, I don't know about this Alpha course. It didn't seem to cut much ice when we did it. I

don't think we'll bother on another occasion.' That's very short-sighted. It's a bit like regarding the carburettor and the steering wheel as optional extras in driving, and then wondering why the car does not get very far.

The meal

Let me explain about the importance of both of these elements in the course, and in life in general. The value of the meal is great. For one thing people are attracted by anything that gives a bit of joy and celebration in life. The meal, if it is well cooked and lovingly presented, does just that. For another, people relax much more during and after a good meal, and are much more prepared to relate to others in the group, to take on board new ideas, to ask honest questions, and generally to enter into the programme in a wholehearted way. They are also much more open to laughter. And laughter, as the *Reader's Digest* discovered long ago, is one of the best medicines in life. You may have noticed the particular gift which Nicky Gumbel has in telling jokes and making folk laugh. There is a lot of laughter in any course he teaches. And that is so important. It is not only good communication, but it opens people up to what is going to follow. There is another crucial point in the meal, though. It involves lots of people in the church. It engenders 'body life', which we looked at rather carefully in a previous chapter. It gets members of the congregation to pull together for this enterprise of helping people to find Christ and get established in him. And the guests are softened by the whole thing. They wonder what motivates people in the church to give up many evenings simply in order to provide nice meals for them and then to clear away and wash up afterwards. This simple act of service in which very ordinary people can

share is a powerful pointer to the new life, the new motivation and love, which Christ brings. If you have no meal,
you fail to elicit congregational participation, and you
miss out on amazing the guests with the kindness of the
workers. Nor do you open up members of the group, and
release them from the preoccupations they have brought
with them from their daily work. You do not express the
hospitality of God, which is what evangelism really is.
Your message and your medium do not match in the same
way, if you leave out the meal. It is a short-sighted policy.
It confirms the suspicion outsiders have that Christianity
is all talk; that it is dogma rather than celebration; that it
is boring, straight-laced teaching delivered by the person
up front. It does nothing to open people up to take in new
ideas or to ask uninhibited questions. In a word, if you
miss out the meal you fail to put them at their ease.

The Holy Spirit emphasis

Very well. But why three chapters on the Holy Spirit? Why
so much teaching in the course about him? Why, for
heaven's sake, have a weekend or a day away devoted to
this rather arcane subject? It is all too easy to cut it out.

But hang on a minute. What is all that emphasis on the
Spirit intended to bring about? Something fundamental. A
shift from the head to the heart, from knowing about God
to knowing God. The Holy Spirit is the agent of the
Godhead within the believer. Thoughtful Christians for a
long time have discussed the comparative merits of
Scripture, tradition and reason in Christianity (coupled, in
some circles, with episcopacy). But not nearly enough
attention has been paid to another equally vital area:
experience. If we do not experience God, the rest is all
head stuff. It's all talk and theory. No wonder so many

conferences and training courses do not come alive. No wonder much Christian teaching does not transform lifestyle or stimulate mission. People are often empty inside, even after years of churchgoing. They have the shell of the nut, but not the kernel; the frame, but not the picture. They are like a computer that has no connection to the mains, or a car that has no petrol. That is what we are like spiritually without God's Holy Spirit in our lives. And many Christians do not realise it. They go to church, discuss the others who go, listen a bit to the sermon, approve or disapprove of the music, and come back another time – in many cases less and less frequently. All because they have no 'tiger in the tank' as the old Esso advert used to say. They are not connected up to God's mains electricity. They are ignorant of his Holy Spirit.

Experience in the Christian life

It is because of this massive lack of experience of the living God that Alpha lays such stress on the subject of the Holy Spirit: who he is, what he can do in us, and how he wants to equip us for serving Christ in our generation. I am delighted that Nicky Gumbel has gone to town on the subject. After all, Paul tells us that if we do not have the Holy Spirit we are not Christians (Romans 8:9). He is no optional extra for the pious, no special domain of the charismatics. He is the fundamental essential if we are going to be Christians at all.

I have heard criticism of Alpha on this score of the Holy Spirit from two sources. One is a nominal, traditional source that says in effect, 'So long as you go to church and are a pillar of rectitude in society, why go in for fancy things like the Holy Spirit? We don't appreciate enthusiasm here.' The other criticism comes from Christians who are suspicious of the charismatic movement, its emphasis on spiritual gifts, and the division and unwise practice which are to be seen in charismatic circles from time to time. They do not like the extravagance in praise, with its modern music, new songs, shallow words and frequent repetition. They abhor the tendency to write others off, the naivety, the inclination to ascribe a person's own ideas and intuitions to the Holy Spirit and so forth. And in much of this they are right. But as I re-read Nicky Gumbel's chapters I see nothing to cavil at. There is no sniff of extravagance here. It is sensible, unvarnished New Testament Christianity.

Alpha on the Holy Spirit

What is he saying? His first chapter on the subject deals with who the Holy Spirit is. Involved in the creation of the world, the Holy Spirit was given by God the Father to special people and for special tasks in Old Testament times. John the Baptist predicted that Jesus would baptise people with the Holy Spirit, and it happened at Pentecost. Since then that gift has never been withdrawn. What could be more orthodox as a brief overview of the Spirit than that? There is nothing contentious at all. When Nicky moves on to look at what the Holy Spirit does, he is just as uncontroversial. The Holy Spirit brings us into God's family, builds us up in the family likeness, and gives us an intimacy with God the heavenly Father. He produces lovely fruits of character in the garden of our lives, he unites us with other members of the family of God, and he gives every member of the body of Christ appropriate gifts so that they may fulfil God's purpose in the new community. No problems there, are there?

The third chapter on the subject deals with the very practical question of how we can allow the Holy Spirit to fill our lives and flow from us. Nicky spends some time in considering the Day of Pentecost, when the Spirit first came to live within believers. The disciples were filled with praise. Does that worry you? Do you never get excited when your football team wins? Or when someone in the family gets engaged or married? There is very little danger in most of us suffering from an overdose of emotion. Lack of emotion, lack of feeling, is a much greater danger. Naturally it is wrong to play on people's emotions, but that is not a regular weakness in church life. Nicky quotes a wonderful old friend of mine, Bishop Cuthbert Bardsley: 'The chief danger of the Anglican Church is not delirious emotionalism.' True, is it not?

Much of the rest of the chapter is given over to a consideration of the gift of tongues. Since something like a third of all Christians in the world, from Roman Catholics to Pentecostals, have this gift, it seems worth a few pages! He explains that it is the ability to speak in ways you have not learned. Sometimes it seems to be a language that one has not learned and sometimes it is words of praise or prayer to God which come from deep within, but make no sense in any known language. Nevertheless, they express some of the concerns of the person praying. He points out that this is one of the many forms of prayer; that it is valuable when our own words run out, when we are feeling spiritually cold and dull, when we are under great pressure, when we are praying for others but do not know what to pray for them, and when our hearts are bursting with love and praise. Nicky makes it very clear that this praying in tongues is not the definitive mark of being filled with God's Holy Spirit. Indeed, it is clear from the letters to Corinth in the New Testament that although the Christians there spoke in tongues they were very unspiritual, and the Holy Spirit clearly did not fill them. He makes it clear that you are no better or worse whether you have this gift or not, but that it is rude to God and foolish for us to turn our back on any of God's gifts. He knows what he is doing. He knows whom to distribute his gifts to and when. Finally Nicky points to doubt, fear and a sense of inadequacy as the main reasons why people fail to receive this gift which the Lord may be wanting to give them.

For the life of me, I can see nothing wrong in all this. Nicky does not suggest that this is a gift for all Christians, or that you cannot be a spiritual Christian without it. It is no divine tick in the margin for the recipient. It is just one of God's many gifts, and because it is one which is regarded by many in the church with ignorance, suspicion and fear he spends some time on it. If I were to criticise the teaching I would want to say that he leaves out a lot about other gifts the Holy Spirit wants to equip his people with – but then you can't do everything, even in three chapters on the subject! There is nothing exclusively 'charismatic' about his teaching. Nothing to raise your temperature. Simply a cool and sane exposition of what part of the New Testament teaches on an important issue. All churches profess to regard the New Testament highly. Nicky Gumbel simply tells us the essence of what it says.

Why the opposition?

I think the real opposition comes from the fact that the Western world is still caught up deeply in the attitudes of the Enlightenment (which we will glance at later). We don't mind worshipping God so long as we can understand it all and can call the shots. But we can't have God barging in with a tongue or a prophecy or a healing. This is not acceptable. It is too threatening. We can't rationalise it. We can't get it under our control. Definitely dangerous!

That, I am sure, is why some Christians try to get rid of it by calling it emotionalism. In fact, praying in tongues is not an emotional experience at all; far less is it what one modern translation renders as 'tongues of ecstasy'. Others try to get out of it by telling us that these gifts we read about in the New Testament all died out at the end of the apostolic age. That is sheer moonshine and betrays culpable ignorance. I have had occasion to read almost all of the Christian literature surviving from the second century and most from the third. The fact is that these gifts did not die out at all. They never have. But there has been a massive resurgence of them in our own day, starting with the emergence of the Pentecostals in 1900, and spreading since then through all the denominations, despite much official opposition. No door can keep the Spirit of God out, so it is best not to try! Much better to take a careful look at what the Bible teaches on this thrilling and important subject, and to live accordingly.

The Spirit in Scripture

The Old Testament tells us a good deal about the Holy Spirit. The most important thing is that it is God we are talking about – God and his invading presence into the world he has made. The Spirit of God comes upon particular people like Gideon and Samson to bring deliverance to his people. He often equips kings and prophets for their task. There were three great disadvantages in those days. First, the Spirit was not for everyone, but for particular people. Second, he could be withdrawn. And third, the Spirit is seen not so much in personal terms as in God's naked power breaking in.

The great prophets like Jeremiah and Ezekiel looked forward to the day when God's Spirit would live in the hearts of all his people, and they would all know the Lord. And instead of God's law being something external to people, telling them what to do, his Spirit would put God's law within their hearts and they would both want to please him and be empowered to do so (Jeremiah 31:31ff; Ezekiel 36:25f).

Those longings were partly fulfilled in the ministry of Jesus. He was the one who was full of the Spirit from his mother's womb. His baptism stressed it. His ministry showed it. There is actually so little about the Holy Spirit in the Gospels because that Spirit was acting through Jesus, the man of the Spirit. And when he is about to leave them and die Jesus gives them much teaching about the Holy Spirit (see John 14:16–18, 25–27; 15:26–27; 16:7–11). He would be Jesus' other self, so to speak. Jesus would be with them in the unseen form of the Holy Spirit as really as when he walked with them down the streets of the Holy Land. That Spirit would bring to their remembrance what Jesus had taught them. He would guide them, give them his own joy and peace, stand with them and be their encourager. He would be their secret weapon in world mission, for he would act as prosecuting counsel, and would convict people of the sin of rejecting Jesus. He would convince them that Jesus was right after all: he had been raised from the dead and had returned to his Father in heaven. And the Spirit would face people up to the fact that they had to decide about him. The great enemy Satan had been given a thorough defeat through the cross and resurrection. People would have to decide whether they were going to commit themselves to Christ the conqueror or not.

The decisive moment came at Pentecost. Jesus had ascended back to heaven and had given the precious gift of his Holy Spirit to all who would have him. No longer confined to the body of Jesus, his unseen self, his Spirit was free to actually come and live in the hearts and lives of the disciples. And the three great snags of Old Testament days were gone. No longer was the Spirit sub-personal, naked power – he was henceforth the Spirit of Jesus. No longer would he be withdrawn, as he was from Samson and Gideon and Saul in Old Testament times. And no longer was he reserved for special people. The hopes of the prophets had been fulfilled, and he was available for all who would welcome him into their lives, be they Jewish or Gentile, male or female, young or old. A new age had dawned with the coming of the Spirit.

The Spirit in mission

Christ's commission

It is abundantly obvious that when the Holy Spirit came on the disciples they changed dramatically. No longer were they a terrified little group huddled in an upstairs room: they were vibrant, confident and out on the streets with the good news of a God who could rescue human beings from the consequences of their evil deeds and could fill empty hearts with his joy and power. It is plain from the first page of Acts that this was the purpose of Jesus. When the Spirit came, the disciples were to bear witness to Jesus, first in Jerusalem and then in ever-widening circles throughout the world (Acts 1:8). The rest of the book shows precisely that happening. First in Jerusalem, then in Judea, then among the Samaritans with whom there had been bad relationships for centuries, then to a representative of the hated Roman invaders, then out of Palestine altogether into Antioch in Syria. From there the mission took off throughout the Roman Empire. I think Acts is the most thrilling book in the world. It shows how in the first generation of Christian witness the believers

spread the good news literally throughout the known world. This was not due to human planning. The apostles themselves seem to have operated mainly in Jerusalem. The mission was carried out by ordinary Christians armed with the extraordinary power of the Spirit of God. It is not so much the Acts of the Apostles as the Acts of the Holy Spirit that we read about in Luke's second volume.

Mission

This raises a most important point. The Holy Spirit was never given to make us comfortable, but to make us witnesses; not to give us an easy time in church, but to make us effective in the wider world. How tragically some sections of the church have failed to act on this down the centuries. Alas, the failure continues in many places today. If Christians talk at all about the Holy Spirit, it is in terms of personal comfort and encouragement. The New Testament regards the initial purpose of his coming as power for witness-bearing. The Spirit bears witness, and the Christians also bear witness (John 15:26–27). It is a tandem relationship, a partnership to bring the gospel to those who lack it. There is always an outward thrust about the Holy Spirit.

Testimony

The Holy Spirit gives great power to simple testimony. All the first Christians are 'witnesses to these things, and so is the Holy Spirit whom God has given to those who obey him' (Acts 5:32). The witness shares his own experience of the Lord. He does not necessarily preach. Acts is full of examples of Christians telling of the difference Christ has made to them, to governors and soldiers, princelings and mediums, crowds and individuals. Witness in the New Testament is neither the silent churchgoing that passes for witness among many Christians, nor the sickening self-advertisement that sometimes results when a believer 'gives his testimony'. It is simple, factual reference to Jesus, his death and resurrection, the gift of his Spirit and his present availability and power. And that is the key to the great growth of the church in Latin America today, particularly among the Pentecostals. Or in African countries like Kenya and Uganda, and, despite persecution, Nigeria and Sudan. Humble Christians are fearless in telling others of the difference Jesus has made to their lives, and the Holy Spirit takes it home to the hearts of the hearers. Others are challenged to make the experiment for themselves, and the church grows.

Proclamation

But Jesus does not promise the aid of his Spirit merely to this informal witness, but also to the more formal proclamation of the word. 'The word' is common in the book of Acts. It means the message about Jesus. The heart of this message has been summarised by some of the best scholars in recent years as follows:

> The age of fulfilment has dawned. This has taken place through the ministry, death and resurrection of Jesus of Nazareth. By virtue of the resurrection Jesus has been raised to the right hand of God and the gift of the Holy Spirit in the church is evidence of his present power and glory. The end of all history will come with the return of Jesus Christ. Hence the importance of repentance, faith and baptism into his church. So receive God's offer of forgiveness and of the Holy Spirit.

This insight came from C. H. Dodd, the most distinguished British New Testament scholar this century. You might care to read his brilliant short book on the subject, *The Apostolic Preaching and Its Development*. Other scholars have added various footnotes to this basic reconstruction of the early Christian preaching, but nobody doubts that this was the essence of their message. This was the word that they preached, and 'we impart this in words not taught by human wisdom but taught by the Spirit' writes Paul to his converts in Corinth (1 Corinthians 2:13). As he recalls bringing the gospel to them in the first place, he reflects, 'I decided to know nothing among you except Jesus Christ and him crucified. And I was with you in weakness and in much fear and trembling; and my speech and my message were not in plausible words of wisdom, but in demonstration of the Spirit and power, that your faith might not rest in the wisdom of men but in the power of God' (1 Corinthians 2:2–5).

If we wonder what the role of the Spirit is in Christian proclamation we do not have far to look. The Spirit convicts a person of sin and makes Jesus attractive to him or her (John 15:26; 16:14). The penny drops, so to speak, and the person realises the truth of what he has heard; and Jesus is revealed as the one who makes sense of everything. Sometimes this happens over a long period, as people find themselves drawn to a place of Christian worship or friendship with Christians. Sometimes it is very sudden. I remember an English university lecturer coming up to me after a meeting and telling me that the scales had fallen from her eyes that night as she listened. She had suddenly seen that Jesus was the answer to the rather negative existentialist framework within which she had hitherto been living. That was the work of the Spirit revealing Christ to her. You see, it is the Spirit who brings a person to faith. You can't do it, nor can I. Only God can reveal God. Nobody can say from the heart that 'Jesus is Lord' without the Holy Spirit enabling them to do so (1 Corinthians 12:3). You see many graphic examples of that in Acts, notably Cornelius, the Roman centurion. As

Peter tells him the good news of Jesus the Spirit falls on him even before Peter has presented the challenge (Acts 10:34–48)! I have seen that happen several times in my own evangelistic ministry. The Spirit loves to illuminate the message and take it home to people's hearts. That is his special function in mission.

The Spirit in the individual

The Spirit, of course, plays an enormous part in making a person a Christian, helping them to grow, and in due course making them like Christ. Let's look at these in turn.

The Spirit in Christian initiation

We have already seen that no one person can make another person a Christian. No parent, no friend, no priest. This is the work of God alone. It is the Spirit who baptises a person into Christ (1 Corinthians 12:13). It is the Spirit who comes and makes his dwelling in our hearts (Romans 8:11). It is the Spirit who brings about the new birth into God's family (John 3:8). It is the Spirit who assures us we belong, and enables us to address the heavenly Father with the same intimate cry as Jesus did, calling him 'Abba, dear Daddy' (Romans 8:15). The Spirit comes and takes up residence within us and our bodies become his temple (1 Corinthians 6:19). Very well, what does he do?

He makes us confident that we belong. That is our Christian birthright. There are five lovely images of this relationship which the New Testament gives us. One is 'adoption' (Galatians 4:5; Ephesians 1:5) Once we were not in God's family. Now we are, adopted alongside Jesus himself.

The second word is 'seal'. Paul tells the Ephesians that they have been sealed by God's Holy Spirit (Ephesians

1:13). 'Seal' is a property word. It speaks of belonging. The Spirit is given to identify us as Christ's property, just as a seal on a letter identifies it as mine.

Another word which Paul uses is 'guarantee' (Ephesians 1:14; 2 Corinthians 5:5). If 'seal' is a property word, 'guarantee' is more prophetic. It looks forward to a greater gift in the future while stressing a real gift in the present. Often used in commerce for a 'down payment' or 'first instalment', it is highly appropriate for the Holy Spirit. He is God's first instalment of the future salvation which awaits us – the bit of the future which we have now. Not surprising that the word is used in Modern Greek for an engagement ring!

The fourth word is 'firstfruits' (Romans 8:23). This is a word from farming. If the firstfruits are good, you can be sure the main crop will be. Christ's resurrection is seen as the firstfruits of our own (1 Corinthians 15:20), and the Holy Spirit is the firstfruits of that harvest God has in store for us.

The final word is 'assurance' (1 Thessalonians 1:5). Paul reminds his readers that the gospel came to them not in word only but in power and in the Holy Spirit and much assurance. The word for 'assurance' literally means being so full that you overflow. That describes the conviction the Spirit gives to our hearts that we really belong. So although there is so much we do not understand, and although we have to walk by faith not by sight in this life, the Holy Spirit is given to us as individuals in order to bring a quiet and deep confidence that we do really belong to the Lord, in spite of all our failures and weaknesses.

The Spirit in Christian growth

The second great area where we may expect to see the Spirit at work in our individual lives is our character. Paul, once again, gives us the best insight into it. He uses the imagery of a garden. Once the Holy Spirit is welcomed into the soil of our lives, a lovely crop begins to grow. He calls it the fruit of the Spirit: 'The fruit of the Spirit is love, joy, peace, patience, kindness, goodness, faithfulness, gentleness and self-control. . . . Those who belong to Christ Jesus have crucified the sinful nature with its passions and desires. Since we live by the Spirit, let us keep in step with the Spirit' (Galatians 5:22–25, NIV).

The apostle is contrasting what he calls 'the acts of the sinful nature' – and a pretty horrific list he gives us – with this 'fruit of the Spirit'. The contrast is absolute, but alas our performance is not. The Holy Spirit will indeed grow his attractive fruit in our lives. But we must not hinder him by deliberately holding on to what is wrong. We should ask the Lord to nail our old unregenerate character onto his cross and progressively to exhibit the lovely fruit of his character in us. It is the task of the Holy Spirit to bring this about.

There is an old saying that in each heart there is a crown and a cross. If my old selfish nature with all its sinful tendencies is calling the shots, then Jesus to all intents and purposes remains on the cross. But if I deliberately ask him to wear the crown in my life and direct my desires and my actions, then he can be relied on to keep that troublesome old nature in the place where it belongs, the place of death. It is all part of the dying and rising life to which our baptism pointed long ago, but it has to be deliberately undertaken day by day. And then we shall not see a bit of patience appearing in one person and a bit of joy in another. No, the whole thing is a *crop*. It is a crop of Christlike qualities which the Spirit is charged to bring about in our lives. To a greater or lesser extent all those qualities will gradually begin to be seen in us Christians.

It will not all happen at once in our spiritual lives, any more than it does in nature. As I write and look out of the window I see crocuses smiling at me. Soon there will be daffodils, then tulips, and later on the whole range of summer glory. I am confident of that, because I already see the crocuses. We can be just as confident about spiritual flowers and fruit in our lives. If we have welcomed the Holy Spirit in, and if we daily ask the Lord to crucify the old nature with its wrong desires, and keep in step with the Spirit and his promptings, the crop of his qualities will assuredly grow in our lives. We may not be particularly conscious of it ourselves, but other people will notice the change. That is what the Holy Spirit will do in Christian lives that remain pliant and sensitive to him. It is wonderful.

There is a staggering claim made in the letter to the Ephesians (1:19–20). It amounts to this. The very power which raised Jesus Christ from the grave on the first Easter Day is at work in Christians through the indwelling Holy Spirit. Paul prays that his readers may be able to take in God's 'incomparably great power for us who believe. That power is like the working of his mighty strength, which he exerted in Christ when he raised him from the dead and seated him at his right hand in the heavenly realms' (NIV). Just think of that. The very power which brought Jesus back from death is available for our lives. We can all tap into it if the Spirit has taken up residence in our hearts. So there is no excuse for saying, 'It's a habit I can't break.' That may well be true humanly speaking. But nothing is too hard for the Lord. The one who raised Christ from the dead can be trusted to break particular chains which shackle us, as well as gradually to grow lovely fruit in our lives. I find that enormously encouraging in my struggles.

The Spirit and Christlikeness

This brings us to the third thing which the Holy Spirit longs to achieve within us. It is to make us Christlike. Think again about that list of qualities we have just glanced at: 'love, joy, peace . . .' and the rest. What are they but a description of the character of Jesus? Think of that famous chapter, 1 Corinthians 13, with its paean to love: 'Love is patient, love is kind. It does not envy, it does not boast, it is not proud. It is not rude, it is not self-seeking, it is not easily angered, it keeps no record of wrongs. Love does not delight in evil but rejoices with the truth. It always protects, always trusts, always hopes, always perseveres' (NIV). Now try putting your own name there instead of 'love'. I could not possibly say, 'Michael is patient, Michael is kind. Michael does not envy, does not boast, is not proud . . .' and so on. It would be ludicrous. But it is very easy to substitute the name of Jesus for 'love'. It is a perfect description of who he is and how he behaves. 'Jesus is patient and kind. He does not envy or boast. He is not rude, self-seeking or easily angered. He keeps no record of wrongs . . .' and so on to the end of that marvellous description. It fits him like a glove. Well, the God who calls us to be recognisable followers of Jesus also offers us the means to make this goal more attainable. True holiness is becoming more and more like Christ, and the Holy Spirit is concerned to bring it about.

There is an illuminating passage at the end of 2 Corinthians 3. Paul is giving his readers a history lesson. When Moses, during Israel's wanderings in the Sinai desert, went into 'the tent of meeting' to spend time with God, his face shone as he came out. This embarrassed the Israelites, and so he veiled his face, partly so that they should not be dazzled, and partly so that they should not see the glow fading! Paul regards that as a picture of Christian reality. The Spirit of the Lord is intent on freeing us up entirely: 'And we, who with unveiled faces all reflect the Lord's glory, are being transformed into his likeness with ever-increasing glory, which comes from the Lord, who is the Spirit' (NIV). The word translated 'reflect' is fascinating. It can either mean 'look into a mirror' or else 'use a mirror to reflect', rather as naughty little boys flash mirrors into the eyes of their teachers! I suspect Paul wants us to see both meanings in the word as he uses it here. As we look into the Scriptures (which is what he is talking about in the context) we will 'behold' our Lord there. And as we leave, we will 'reflect' something of his glory. Moses did, but it faded. Under the hand of the Holy Spirit, however, it will increase and we shall gradually be changed from one degree of 'reflecting' Jesus (as a mirror reflects the sun) to another. That is a mind-boggling prospect, but our God expects no less from us, and the Spirit makes it possible.

Those seem to be the main areas which the Holy Spirit is concerned with in the individual Christian life. He wants us to be sure that we belong. He wants us to grow in character. He wants us to become more and more like Christ. And two important avenues towards that goal are prayer and guidance.

The Spirit and prayer

If you are anything like me, you will not find prayer coming easily. God understands about that, and expressly provides the Spirit to help us in our prayer life. We read of Christians 'praying in the Spirit' (Jude 20; Ephesians 6:18). This seems to indicate times when the Spirit gives us great freedom in our prayers and praises. Those who have taken part in whole nights of prayer will recall times when the Spirit takes over and you can go on praying for hours without noticing the passage of time – and then be wide awake and invigorated (although sleepless) the next morning as you go to work.

Another way in which the Holy Spirit helps us in our prayers is outlined in Romans 8:26–28: 'The Spirit helps us in our weakness; for we do not know how to pray as we ought, but the Spirit himself intercedes for us with sighs too deep for words. And he who searches the hearts of men knows what is the mind of the Spirit, because the Spirit intercedes for the saints according to the will of God. We know that in everything God works for good with those who love him.'

The Spirit and guidance

Guidance is a constant puzzle for most of us. We want to go God's way, but we are perplexed as to what it is. There is no easy answer, and I think I have found it more difficult as I have got older – maybe by now God trusts me to have gained sufficient insight into the general mind of Christ to make decisions wisely, without his special intervention. I don't know. But I am very grateful for the sensible way in which my friend the late David Watson drew from the Bible four strands in divine guidance which together provide us with a confident basis for action. They save us from the pious, unanswerable but often misguided claim you find in some enthusiastic new Christians: 'The Lord told me to do such and such.' Here they are.

First, God guides us through the Scriptures. The Spirit who inspired them in the first place is well able to make some part of them impact us so strongly that it becomes an inescapable pointer to a particular course of action. To pick a verse at random from Scripture proves nothing at all, except that we are not using the Bible properly. Let us rather follow Paul's advice: 'Let the word of Christ dwell in you richly, as you teach and admonish one another in all wisdom' (Colossians 3:16). An increasingly broad appreciation of the Scriptures will give us a developing ability to sense the will of God in a given situation.

Second, God guides through other Christians and their sensible advice, as he did in Acts 6 when the whole multitude chose the Seven, or in Acts 13 when the Spirit spoke to the church at Antioch about the need for Paul and Barnabas to go abroad on mission. Personal convictions should be open to testing by the guidance of other Christians.

Third, God guides us in prayer. David Watson used to point to Colossians 3:15, 'Let the peace of Christ rule [i.e. be the decision-maker] in your hearts.' Pray until you have peace about a course of action, and then go with it.

And fourth, God guides through circumstances (Acts 16:10). God closes some doors and opens others. It is our responsibility to remain alert and follow through the doors when they open.

By all these means the Holy Spirit can give us the help

in guidance that we so badly need.

These are some of the ways of the Spirit in the life of the individual Christian. If, through Alpha and elsewhere, we have learned a bit of what it means to 'keep in step with the Spirit' it is our responsibility to live out that kind of life in our church, our home and our place of work.

The Spirit in the church

The Spirit of Jesus is profoundly concerned for his church. This is brought out very strongly in the New Testament.

The Spirit creates unity in the church

When Paul is outlining the bonds of Christian unity in Ephesians 4:3–4 he says: 'Endeavour to keep the unity of the Spirit in the bond of peace. There is one body, and one Spirit, as you are called in one hope of your calling.' We can't make peace, but we certainly can wreck it! He is the peacemaker; we must endeavour to keep the unity he creates in Christ. As we saw earlier, Christ's church is meant to display that diversity in unity which marks a healthy human body. And the power, the vitality if you like, which produces that is the Holy Spirit. The apostle reminds them that they are called collectively to be Christ's body, diverse but united, throbbing with the life of the Spirit. In his own day the Spirit brought Jews and Gentiles, men and women, old and young, rich and poor, owners and slaves together in a unity which amazed the ancient world. Today, people scoff at Christian denominations with their absurd divisions, and make that an excuse for keeping well clear of an organisation which appears so small-minded and divided. What a tragic reversal of Christ's purpose! You have sensed real Christian unity in your Alpha course, have you not? Then show it, and work for unity and partnership, love and mutual respect in the church where you belong. Always be on the side that unites rather than divides the body of Christ. Make that one of your aims. Be a man or woman of peace. That is meant to be a lovely work of the Spirit through you.

The Spirit fosters reconciliation in the church

Reconciliation is closely allied to unity. Many churches are rendered powerless despite large numbers, good preaching and so forth, because they are full of unreconciled squabbles and divisions. To be sure, these are concealed beneath smiling Sunday faces, but they are only papered over, and our Lord has X-ray eyes. The Spirit of the Lord cannot shine out from a community if it is fractured with divisions (Ephesians 2:22). Earlier in that chapter Paul has given a graphic example of what he means. Jews and Gentiles were terribly divided in antiquity. There was a great high wall in the temple keeping non-Jews out. Paul tells his readers that Christ's death has changed all that for ever. His death has brought near those who were far off. He is our peace. He has made both estranged parties one. He has broken down that wall which spelled hostility between them. His purpose is to create a new humanity, with warring factions reconciled to one another and to God through the cross. Then we both have access to the Father through the Spirit.

That is what it is all about. So if there are people you have wronged in the congregation, why not go and apologise to them, even if they (not you) have been the main cause of the trouble? You never lose by being the first to apologise. And if you have felt the vicar really is not up to much, and have said so, why not go and offer to be of some service in the work of the church? That is how the Lord can shine out from the Christian community. It is not the place which is faultless – far from it. But it is the place where forgiveness is offered and received and where reconciliation flows. And that is a beacon of light in a sorely divided world.

The Spirit creates fellowship in the church

You know how we so often end services with 'May the grace of our Lord Jesus Christ and the love of God and the fellowship of the Holy Spirit be with us all evermore'? It comes from 2 Corinthians 13:14. The phrase may mean 'the fellowship which the Spirit gives', or 'joint participation in the Holy Spirit'. While both are true, the latter is the more profound. If we are Christians at all, we share in the first instalment and pledge of the age to come, the Holy Spirit. That gives us an essential bond with all others who have received him. So it is important to let that sharing have practical expression. Meals together, work parties, houseparties, forms of outreach – these all enable us to feel that real sense of belonging which is one of the glories of Christianity. I find it amazing that wherever I go all over the world (and I travel a lot) I find this fellowship awaiting me.

Just recently I stayed with an admiral and his wife in a foreign land. They knew neither me nor anything about me, but they heard I was coming to their church and immediately offered hospitality. They drove for an hour to collect me, made me thoroughly welcome and took every possible care of me as we talked and prayed and rejoiced together. We are now fast friends. That is one of the precious gifts of the Spirit. You will have experienced something of it in Alpha. So try to foster it wherever you are among Christians. St John sees this as a surpassing demonstration that we really are Christians and have passed from death to life – when we love one another (1 John 3:14). I have found that once you start praying with people you break through to that unity in the Spirit which underlies all the common courtesies, and you find a depth of fellowship that is hard to describe but rich to enjoy. I think we often rob ourselves of it because we do not pray together.

The Spirit enriches worship in the church

The Day of Pentecost resounded with praise and worship once the Spirit came upon the disciples. And he loves to enrich the worship of God's people. Jesus told the Samaritan woman that the worship acceptable to God was not necessarily pretentious and perfectly executed liturgies, but worship that was real and lit up by the Spirit (John 4:23–24). God is actually looking for people to worship him that way, according to Jesus. And he should know. So the croaking song of a real believer may reach God in heaven, while the perfect anthem of an unspiritual choir gets no further than the ceiling.

That is not to say we should be careless about quality in our worship. Quite the reverse. Nothing is too good for God. But we should get our priorities straight. We need to have our hearts open to God, our inner eyes concentrating on him, our hands open to receive from him, our love flowing to him. When much of the congregation is worshipping in that attitude the Spirit has a way of making himself known almost physically. You know he is there. The Scriptures speak with power, because the Spirit who inspired them takes them and applies them to sensitive hearts. The praise lingers. Nobody wants to leave, because they know they are in the presence of the Holy One. I have known services when I have gone to the back to greet worshippers as they emerged, and for ten minutes or more nobody moved: there was a silence which could be felt, and yet several hundred people were present. I can think of another time when praise began to emerge spontaneously and people were lost in wonder, love and praise.

There are other aspects of the service which the Spirit enlivens. The preaching is one: it may be very pedestrian in style and composition, but when the Holy Spirit is active it reaches through to hearts and people say, 'I felt you were speaking to me personally.' We read of one of the early addresses in Acts: 'Then Peter, filled with the Holy Spirit, said . . .' (Acts 4:8). That address had exceptional power. So when you are given opportunities to preach, drench your preparation in prayer and dependence on the Holy Spirit. If someone else is preaching, you might like to agree with a few friends to pray for him during the sermon itself. The Spirit of God loves to use the preached message, and it is one of the prime ways of building up a congregation and speaking to the hearts of those who come in for the first time.

In the same way the Spirit brings life and power to the sacraments. Probably there is an allusion to baptism in John 3:5, 'born of water and the Spirit', and to the Eucharist in John 6:53, 'unless you eat the flesh of the Son of man and drink his blood, you have no life in you'. If so, it can hardly be accidental that the Spirit is mentioned prominently in both places. The water, the bread and the wine by themselves can avail little. It is the Spirit which gives life to them. Jesus said as much in John 6:63, 'It is the spirit that gives life, the flesh is of no avail.' The Spirit is vital to effective baptism that unites a person to Christ and to meaningful Communion that feeds a person on him. That says a lot about the attitude we need to adopt as we come to the sacraments.

The Spirit offers gifts for the church

The last thirty years have seen a great deal of debate about the so-called charismatic gifts. They engender wild enthusiasm in some, and fierce opposition in others. I have written carefully on the whole subject in my book *I Believe in the Holy Spirit* (Hodder & Stoughton). And you have looked into the matter during your Alpha course. The Spirit furnishes each of us with various gifts, to be used not for our private gratification but for the good of Christ's church.

The key passage of Scripture on the topic is 1 Corinthians 12–14. Paul wrote these three chapters because of trouble at Corinth. They were rich in spiritual gifts, but they clearly prized the impressive ones like speaking in tongues, miracles, healing and prophecy more than the apparently pedestrian ones like gifts of administration and helping others. Paul was not impressed by this spiritual apartheid.

Important preliminaries

First, he reminds them of their pagan days and the frenzies they got into when worshipping idols. It seems that something of the sort may have happened in worship at Corinth. People were apparently shouting, *'Anathema Iesous'*, 'Jesus be cursed' (12:3). Paul sharply rebukes them and reminds them that contrary to bizarre cries being the mark of the Spirit's inspiration, you cannot make the most basic baptismal confession, 'Jesus is Lord', without the Holy Spirit prompting you. He wants them to know that every Christian has the Spirit – not just some specially gifted ones. He makes the same point in verse 13 when he says, 'By one Spirit we were all baptized into one body – Jews or Greeks, slaves or free – and all were made to drink of one Spirit.' They would not have liked that at all. It hit at the sense of superiority that some of them had because of their particular gifting. So Paul makes another crucial point: all the gifts that any Christians have are the result of careful apportionment by the Holy Spirit. He knows what he is doing in the body of Christ, and he gives to all of us appropriate gifts. So three things are plain. These gifts are varied. These gifts are provided by the Holy Spirit, not dished out by some charismatic speaker. And they are not for anyone to crow about – they are 'for the common good' (12:7). Paul wants to rub that point in. He makes it again when continuing this discussion in chapter 14. These abilities are given 'so that the church may be edified' (14:5). They are for 'building up the church' (14:12).

Gifts of utterance

What, then, are these gifts? The list he gives here of nine gifts is not exhaustive. There is a different list at the end of this chapter 12, and yet another in Romans 12. He is clearly just giving us some examples of how the Spirit gifts and empowers people.

He mentions three gifts of utterance: tongues, interpretation of tongues and prophecy. Nicky Gumbel speaks sensibly about the gift of tongues in his video and the book. It is primarily designed for communication with God in prayer and praise (14:2), in a vocabulary one has not learned. Generally it is incomprehensible to the person praying, but is valuable all the same: it builds up the user, and we all need that (14:4). Sometimes, these chapters make clear, it can be of use in congregational worship if, and only if, it is interpreted. Otherwise our spirit may pray but our mind has not a clue what is going on (14:14). That is why Paul encourages people to pray for the complementary gift of interpretation (14:13). This is not a word-for-word equivalent to what has been said in a tongue, but the ability to interpret the sense of it.

The third gift of utterance, which Paul valued very highly, is prophecy. This is not necessarily prediction, but it is speaking a short message directly from God into a particular situation. It is inspired by the Holy Spirit, just as Scripture is, but it does not have the same authority as Scripture. Nor does it have the same universal scope. A prophetic utterance today is meant for one particular situation rather than for the universal church down the centuries. It is valuable because it is direct and intelligible, unlike tongues, though Paul allows that tongues plus interpretation comes to much the same thing (14:5). A series of very shrewd caveats is found in this chapter. Here are some questions to ask in the presence of a putative prophecy.

First, does it glorify God (14:25)? If it glorifies the speaker or a denomination or whatever, forget it. Second, is it in accord with Scripture (14:37ff)? The God who inspired Scripture is not going to contradict it through a prophecy. If it is unscriptural we may safely discard it. Third, does the supposed prophecy build up the church (14:5)? If not, it has not come from God. Fourth, is it spoken with love (14:1)? Prophecy is one of God's love gifts. Fifth, does the speaker submit to the judgement and consensus of others (14:29)? Or is he or she authoritarian and unteachable? Sixth, is the speaker in control of himself (14:32)? Prophecy, like tongues, is neither uncontrollable nor ecstatic. Order is one of the signs of God's presence (14:40). Finally, is there too much of it (14:29ff)? The longer a speaker goes on the more likely he is to have confused his own ideas with God's word.

In ways like this Paul controls but does not forbid the

use of this valuable spiritual gift. Prophets were highly regarded in the early church, and it is sad that the use of this particular gift seems to be restricted to certain kinds of churches these days. It could be valuable for all.

If you think God has gifted you in one of these ways, it would probably be wise to test it in a small group of loving friends. Only when you are very confident that it is a genuine gift from God should you approach your minister and offer it for occasional use in church. It need cause no disorder. When I was a parish priest we had prophetic messages from time to time as God gave pictures or direct words for the edification of the congregation. On one occasion it happened in the presence and with the active participation of the then Archbishop of Canterbury. He was not in the least phased!

Gifts of action

Next in his lists of nine examples Paul mentions, without explaining, three gifts of action: healing, miracles and faith. We can deal with these more briefly since, surprisingly, they cause less controversy.

Healing is a vital part of the ministry of the church today, as it was in Jesus' own ministry. Most churches have prayers for the sick during their intercessions, and many have special prayer services for healing. In some cases there seems to be no expectation of anyone getting healed; it just makes people feel better to come and pray. Well, there is value in that. To bring our needs to God, even without any expectation that he might do something about them, can't be bad. But how much better if those prayers are offered in the expectancy that healing does happen today.

Nicky Gumbel has a whole chapter on the subject, and I do not want to add much to it. Simply to say that when

I was a young man I doubted whether God did in fact heal today, and I am glad to say I was wrong. I have seen and been part of many healings during my ministry – spiritual, psychosomatic, relational and physical. God may use any member of his body to convey healing in a particular instance. I remember my first vicar's experience. His son had a dreadful accident and was told he would never walk again. His father laid hands on him and prayed, and he was wonderfully healed and continued hale and hearty for many years. But my vicar was never used in that way again! Some find themselves being channels of divine healing quite often, and these are called 'healers' in 1 Corinthians 12:28. It might be right for you to ask God if this is a ministry he has for you. But never forget that God's main way of healing is through the medical profession. He can bring healing without medicine, and does so at times, but normally works through the doctors. Thank God for them! And do not imagine that it is somehow holier to be healed through prayer than through antibiotics. The same God is at work through both.

'Miracles' is obscure, and in English it sounds very improbable. In the original it means simply 'acts of power'. I personally believe it to refer to the deliverance of people from satanic power which can bind them. It is sometimes called exorcism, though this word should be reserved for the most serious cases. Normally it is 'deliverance ministry', setting people free from being affected by one or more of the three main forms of the occult: magic, fortune-telling and spiritism. You need to be very careful before engaging in any ministry of this sort. There are a lot of charlatans about for one thing. There are also people with psychological diseases, mental aberrations and spiritual fixations who will tell you they have committed the unforgivable sin and expect you to minister dramatically to them. Be very careful. It is wise to consult the doctor concerned. Do not attempt anything on your own. Go as an apprentice with someone who knows what they are doing. But having said that, demon possession is very common and very obvious in the Two Thirds World. In the West it is not uncommon, but it is much less obvious and often wrongly diagnosed. Years ago it was laughed out of court. Nowadays you will not find many effective clergy who have not had to face it. Never seek to be involved in this stuff. But if you find yourself in a situation where you have to act, challenge whatever evil spirit seems to be troubling the other person, and command it to leave in the name of Jesus Christ. In due course it will, but maybe not before you have had a long battle.

As for the gift of faith, Paul is clearly not talking about the faith you need to become a Christian. He does not mean the ability to trust Jesus Christ for salvation. No, the 'gift of faith' is the sort of thing that drove Noah to build an ark in the middle of a desert plain; that drove a penniless doctor to go as a missionary to China and found the largest missionary society in the world. That was Hudson Taylor in the last century. A more modern example would be Jackie Pullinger, who felt impelled against all advice to go out on her own and without support to the Walled City in Hong Kong. She ministered with great effect among the crooks, pimps and drug addicts of that terrible place, and hundreds have been brought to faith in Christ and a radical change of life. There are people like Jackie who have this special gift of faith, of trusting God in the dark, of betting on the impossible, because they know that is what God wants them to do. And it is to be classed as a gift of action

because they do not just dream these impossible dreams –
they go out and do them!

Gifts of knowledge

The last trio of examples Paul brings before us in this
remarkable chapter concerns the gifts of knowledge. He
calls them a word of wisdom, a word of knowledge and
discrimination (the ability to distinguish) between spiritual things. The last of these is invaluable if any of the gifts
are to be exercised. It is crucial to have someone who has
the ability to tell the difference between, for example,
someone who is praying in a demonic tongue and someone
who is praying in the Spirit. I have actually been in situa-
tions where that has happened, and one is very grateful
indeed for someone with this gift. The same discrimination is an incalculable asset when prophecy is being
offered. If something purports to come from God it is
rather important to know if it is genuine or not!

The gift of discrimination is fairly clear, and immensely
useful. The other two are less clear. But probably a 'word
of wisdom' means advice coming from someone who has
lived close to God for many years and has become wise
and able to help and guide others. The New Testament
does not see this as a sudden or occasional gift at all, but
as the fruit of years of discipleship. It is a settled disposi-
tion of mind, illuminated by the Holy Spirit, which has a
broad understanding of the purposes of God, of the
Scriptures and above all of the Lord himself. That gift is to
be used for the good of people in the church who seek
advice.

The 'word of knowledge' is very different. It seems to
be the ability to have immediate insight into a situation,
almost as if God gives you a word on the subject. Compare
1 Corinthians 13:2 and 14:6 and you will see that Paul is

speaking of some revelatory word from God for the
benefit of others. Jesus clearly had that when he knew that
the woman of Samaria had had five husbands. Peter
clearly had that when he knew that the hearts of Ananias
and Sapphira were not right with God. It is a God-given
disclosure of knowledge which could not normally be
available to the recipient. It is intended not for the gratification of the individual who receives it, but for the
benefit of the whole congregation, or of some member in
it. It is a particularly precious gift for the Christian coun-
sellor, who needs to know the heart of the person with
whom he or she is dealing. But it is a very dangerous gift.
It is so easy to get things wrong and make a disastrous
diagnosis or statement which can do untold harm, backed
up as it is with divine sanctions. Pray that if this ability
comes your way you may be delivered from dangerous mistakes and may be very sensitive in its use.

Implications

What are we to make of all this? If you believe that God is
alive and well today, and that his Spirit is active in the lives
of believers, there is no need to be sceptical about these
gifts. It is sometimes said that they died out long ago. They
did not. They are used today all over the world, in the West
as well as in the East. But you will not want to be hood-
winked or taken for a ride. You will pray for discernment.
You will offer any gift you have with deep humility and in
the knowledge that others may regard it as misguided on
any particular occasion. You will make love your aim, and
you will desire and use these gifts of the Spirit for the
common good, not to earn any spiritual Brownie points
for yourself.

There remain a few issues which we must glance at
before we end this chapter.

Is the distinction between natural and supernatural gifts valid?

The short answer is 'no'. The very word 'gift' or 'charism' (from the Greek *charisma*) is used not only of the gifts such as we have looked at above, but of marriage and singleness in 1 Corinthians 7:7. Indeed, it is used to describe eternal life which awaits all believers (Romans 6:23). So let us have done with this division of Christians into 'charismatics' and 'non-charismatics'. We all belong together in the family of God. Indeed, we are all 'charismatics' in the sense that we all have some gracious gifts (*charismata*) from the Holy Spirit. They may be natural ones like marriage and singleness or whacky-sounding ones like tongues and exorcism. The thing to get clear is that these all come from the same source. They are all endowments by the Spirit to different members of the body for ministry. We are not to be proud of the ones we have, or bewail the ones we do not have. We are to use what we have. We need to remain open to anything new the Lord has for us. And we are to make sure that we deploy all we have for the common good.

What about all this falling over?

A phenomenon has arisen which is called the Toronto Blessing. It came into prominence as part of the spiritual manifestations a few years ago in a small church (which has now become large!) in Toronto. People fell unconscious or semi-conscious as they were prayed for. Sometimes folk stood behind them as 'catchers', but nobody in my experience has ever been hurt falling without a catcher. It is very spectacular when the floor is carpeted with bodies.

The question is, what good does it do, and is it biblical?

Well, nobody is quite sure what good it does. It almost always seems to bring the person a deep sense of the love of the Lord and warms their heart and soul. It is sometimes accompanied by laughter or tears, as deep emotional reservoirs, long repressed, are released by the Holy Spirit. The person concerned usually, though by no means always, knows what God has been doing to them while they have been unconscious. But in churches where this happens (and they are to be found all over the world, including places that have never heard of Toronto) there is usually some spiritual advance connected with the experience.

However, it is not well attested in Scripture. (There people fell on their faces before the Lord in awe and worship on many occasions, but today's people fall on their back.) So it would be quite wrong to regard it as something which should be taught throughout the churches and expected in every congregation. I believe the then Bishop of London (now Archbishop of York), David Hope, hit the nail on the head when he was chatting with me one day: 'I don't mind them falling down. I want to know if they are any good when they get up!' Beat that for sheer wisdom, if you can!

But I don't have any of these gifts!

Oh yes you do. Don't insult God by telling him he did not know what he was doing when he made you 'to the praise of his glorious grace' (Ephesians 1:6). He knew just what he was doing. And he has given you the right equipment – mental, physical and spiritual – to achieve his purpose in and through you. Ask him to show you what your gifts are. Ask your Christian friends – they can often see us much more clearly than we can see ourselves. And when you know what your main gifts are, see how you can use them for the common good – in the home, in the church and in the workplace. That is why God has given them to you, and you will be accountable to him for their use. But don't feel content just to use the gifts you have. Pray to the Lord from time to time that if he wants to give you any other ability he will do so and that you will gratefully accept it from his hand and use it in his service.

9

Life After Alpha

The thrust of this book has been very simple. I have wanted to make a suggestion to readers who have been through the Alpha course (and there are many hundreds of thousands of them) that they should reflect on why the Alpha course has proved so very popular and effective in many countries. I invite them to attempt to isolate the principles lying behind it and to carry them into home, work and church life.

The first chapter was devoted to the issue of real encounter with Jesus Christ. Not religion and discussion, not reading and theology, but encounter. This is what changes lives. We are not going to be able to do it by asking people to come back to church. They won't. Nor will reform of morals cut ice. Think of what happened to 'Back to basics'. If there is to be a resurgence of real Christianity in this country it will not come from the establishment, the schools or the theologians. It will come from ordinary people introducing their friends to Christ, so that they know him for themselves, are sure of it, and have got something to pass on to others. That has always been the heart of authentic Christianity, and Alpha, among other organisations, has majored on it. You do not become a Christian without personal encounter with

Christ. And once you find him, you pass the good news on to others in every way you can. That is a message which desperately needs to be heard in our churches.

The second chapter looked at proper confidence among Christian people, something notably lacking these days in many churchpeople. You cannot build a good house on weak foundations, and you cannot build a useful Christian life on spiritual insecurity. You need to know where you stand with God. The Bible allows us to be confident of this, and Alpha underlines it. The course is turning out many men and women who are confident of their God and are prepared to share him with other people. How else can we expect people to find God except through the testimony of their friends who are already in touch with him?

A highly significant characteristic of modern life is process, preferably accompanied process, and that was the main thrust of Chapter 3. We learn best not by having the handbook thrown at us or by being dropped into a situation and expected to survive, but by somebody coming alongside to show us, to help, to encourage and to be on hand when things go wrong. I know, because I am on the receiving end of an accompanied journey like that, as my son helps his Stone Age father to cope with the computer! I cannot understand the handbook with its special brand of 'computer speak'. I am lost as I look at the laptop and wonder which button to press first. But Tim has spent time with me, trained me, helped me and the result is that I am able at least to write a book on it. And I have him to turn to when chaos strikes. Last night the printer ate great chunks of paper and then staggered to a halt and refused to perform properly thereafter. So I called him. And in the kindness of his heart he was here before breakfast to sort it out. That is what the accompanied journey means to me in the computer scene. Equally in the Christian scene there is a crying need for an accompanied journey of faith, and Alpha has realised it. It is no good these days dropping people from a great height into Christianity, calling for a crisis decision and then leaving them to get on with it. They need the accompanied journey, and that is what Alpha provides. That is a very important principle in Christian nurture, and other courses such as Emmaus are being developed which are based on the accompanied journey. Surely this is so vital that it ought to be carried through into many areas of church life – the leadership of house groups, learning how to preach effectively and so forth. People learn by apprenticeship under good mentors. But from my observation very little of this mentoring is to be seen in Christian circles as yet, though it is increasingly common in secular management structures.

Chapter 4 was devoted to the important topic of personal development and growth in the relationship with Christ, and that again is often neglected in many churches. Clergy assume people in the pew pray, and they may encourage them to read the Bible, but little help is given in either area, and so we see a generation of spiritually anaemic Christians who have neither the motivation nor the knowledge to reach out to a de-Christianised society. Alpha provides both motivation and know-how. Those who have benefited from this training need to pass on what they have learned beyond the structures of Alpha. It is an essential part of nurture.

Chapter 5 was concerned with the much neglected issue of 'every-member ministry'. This is central in the New Testament but little understood in the Western churches, where many members see their responsibility beginning and ending with church attendance on Sunday morning. There will be no revival of Christianity in the West until

we regain the understanding which is so obvious to
Christians in Africa and Asia, that every Christian is a
witness and every Christian has a ministry. The longer we
leave it to a professional priesthood, the speedier will be
our decline. One of the great strengths of Alpha is its
emphasis in theory and practice on shared leadership and
every-member ministry. That is what those who have benefited from Alpha need to try to bring about in their local
church. It is one of the highways to renewal.

Chapter 6 was all about the sacraments, because this
was an important omission in the Alpha course. Chapter
7 developed the theme of Christian discipleship which had
been given an excellent start in Alpha. Needless to say it is
absolutely fundamental. If our lives do not commend
Christ, nobody will listen to what we have to say. And in
general the standard of Christian holiness is not high in
the West. We need to pay serious attention to it if we are
to make any impact on our society which is fed up with
empty words and wants to see real change among those
who claim the name of Christ.

I came across a remarkable example of this only last
weekend: a Christian youth hostel, The Shelter, in the
middle of the Red Light district in central Amsterdam.
Way back in 1855 *Tod Heil des Volks* ('For the salvation of
the people') came into being through the initiative of Jan
de Liefde. He worked as a pastor in the city for many
years, and was moved by the abject poverty and need he
saw all around him. This Dutch inner-city mission has had
a remarkable and flexible ministry down the years since
then. But it has always had two aims: to preach the good
news of Jesus Christ and to give practical help.

Food and clothing were provided for the needy from the
outset. They were taught professional skills and their children were given free schooling. During the Second World

War, while Holland was occupied by the Nazis, they actively helped Jews to escape, and their director spent time in a Nazi prison for his pains. After the war, as Europe was being rebuilt and a new affluence gradually banished poverty from the heart of Amsterdam, the association looked for new ways to fulfil its twin aims. The city was swamped with young people in the heyday of 'flower power' in the late 60s, and drugs and a lack of accommodation became obvious problems.

Accordingly, they set up one drug rehabilitation centre in the city, and two more in the countryside far away from the bright lights, where addicts of various kinds could make a clean break with their old life of prostitution, drug addiction or alcoholism, and start afresh. Large numbers have made a new beginning in life, and lots of them have found Jesus Christ as their Saviour and Lord.

That is not all. Amsterdam draws vast numbers of young people. The hotels are expensive and some of them are dangerous in this city given over to sexual exploitation. So they have deliberately set out to provide hostels for young people travelling through. The one I visited has 166 beds and offers good clean accommodation (the cheapest of its kind in the city) to some 19,000 people a year from all over the world. The staff are all highly motivated Christians. They comprise three managers and a team of volunteers between the ages of twenty and thirty-five who come for six months or a year and work in exchange for accommodation and pocket-money. They seek to express the love of Christ in many ways. They use videos, music, testimonies, Bible studies, drama and personal conversations. They give practical help to the thousands who pass through. And they see a lot of people being drawn to their Lord.

I was very impressed by this place. They run a Scarlet

Cord ministry among the 10,000 prostitutes in the city, offering love and practical care, and helping those who wish to leave prostitution and build a new life. They have a highly effective ministry among the massive homosexual population of the inner city. Those who want to change can come without fear of rejection, and receive loving encouragement, counselling, accommodation and practical help. As a result, many have come to Christian faith, and have found the transforming power of Jesus Christ.

That is the sort of Christianity that cuts ice. That is why Chapter 7 developed the teaching in Alpha about a Christian lifestyle, loyal to Jesus in all areas of life, and ready to meet human need in his name. The more church-people live attractive lives and attempt to meet at least some part of the sea of need around them without asking anything in return, the faster the gospel of Christ will advance. When people who are apathetic about spiritual things see holiness of life and practical love like this, then – and not before – they may sit up and take notice. For there is nothing in the non-Christian world quite like it. It stands out like a beacon.

Our eighth chapter looked at the work of the Holy Spirit. I hope I have been able to give a reasonably balanced summary of at least some of the main points in the Bible's teaching about the third member of the Trinity. There is still a vast amount of prejudice, suspicion and fear whenever the subject of the Holy Spirit comes up. Equally there is a lot of nonsense attributed to him by ill-taught enthusiasts. I believe the three chapters in Nicky Gumbel's book *Questions of Life*, on which the course is based, are both balanced and accurate, and I am glad to have been able to take the subject a little further in this chapter. For of this we can be sure: only a supernatural Christianity, only a faith which takes seriously the Spirit at work in our midst, has any hope of making any impact in the third millennium. Alpha has given a superb lead in that direction. It is now up to you who have been through Alpha to carry out these principles in life after Alpha.

TAILPIECE

For the Culture Vultures

Before we leave the fascinating topic of Alpha and all that flows from it, here is a question you may have been wondering about. Why has Alpha proved so significant in our religious life at this particular juncture in history? It originated in a single London church, Holy Trinity Brompton. From there it has spread to many parts of the world in a very few years, and its growth continues apace. Clearly it has rung a bell. The question is: why? To be sure, it clearly has the blessing of Almighty God upon it. That is very evident. But there are some human reasons as well, and they are well worth investigating. How are we to account for this remarkable phenomenon?

The Christian faith is like an electric current. Its power depends on two terminals through which the current can flow. One of the terminals is the good news proclaimed by Jesus and his apostles and preserved in the New Testament. The other is the appropriate cultural medium of the day. A few examples will illustrate the point.

In the second century AD there were two major cultural terminals. One was the need which so many people felt of being delivered from the demonic pressures which exercised a tyrannical hold on their lives. The other was the need for a way of looking at the world which made sense of the civilisation, culture and knowledge of antiquity, and yet went beyond them. The gospel spoke to each of those concerns, because it proclaimed Christ both as the victor over dark forces, and as the true wisdom.

A little later the cultural terminal which enabled the power to flow was the idea of captivity and ransom. The Christians latched on to this hunger. Through his death on the cross, they maintained, Christ has paid a ransom for the liberation of mankind, and now has the right to install us, sinners though we are, in God's family. The gospel proclaimed Christ as the liberator who has paid the costly ransom.

In the late Middle Ages the issue was one of justification. On what grounds was it possible for sinful man to gain reconciliation with his Maker? The culture of the day said, 'By good deeds, supplemented with penances, indulgences and the prayers of the saints.' But the message of the gospel which brought powerful reformation throughout Europe was that Christ offers full and free justification to all who come to the Father through him, because of his completed work upon the cross. Our standing with God is not something we can earn. It is something God freely gives.

In each case, the gospel spread with all the power of an electric current once the two terminals were in place. Lose either the New Testament gospel or the cultural pressure-point of the day, and there is no spark. Connect the two, and you get power and light.

Very well, how about our own day? It is clear that the Alpha course, with its extraordinary spread all over the world and through almost all denominations in just a few years, has pressed a highly significant button in our own culture. In a sense, what Alpha is doing is not so novel. There have been other induction courses into vital

Christianity, run by many churches. These have some of the same ingredients as Alpha, and yet they have not taken off in anything like the same way. Why should this be? And why did the astonishing success of Alpha not take place thirty years ago, or a century ago for that matter?

The answer must surely lie in the fact that Alpha has managed to make that firm connection between the New Testament gospel and the culture of our day – a culture which is so complex and confusing because it is undergoing very rapid change.

The cultural revolution

We live today at a fascinating time. It is likely to prove one of the great cultural hinges of human history, as significant as when the Stone Age turned into the Bronze Age, or when the Roman Empire was toppled by barbarian tribes. We are in that kind of transition today. 'The old is dying,' remarked Jonathan Sachs, the Chief Rabbi, 'and the new is waiting to be born.'

The 'old' is what we have come to call modernism. It lasted roughly 200 years: if you like, from the fall of the Bastille in 1789 to the fall of the Berlin Wall in 1989. Of course the roots lay much further back, in the Greek humanism which combined with Hebrew–Christian faith to mark off that western part of the continent of Asia which we call Europe, and define its character. But by the end of the eighteenth century many influential thinkers were rejecting the Christian elements in their cultural inheritance, and relegating God to the sidelines. He was despatched to the House of Lords where he could have little influence, and the new Prime Minister would be reason. Human reason was to be the cement to hold society together. The Age of Reason, or the

Enlightenment as it is called, has proved by far the most significant factor in the intellectual development of the world during the past 200 years.

The eighteenth century saw a great intellectual flowering. Scientists like Newton, thinkers like Voltaire, philosophers like Descartes, Locke and Hume – these were the people who set the stage in the new modern age. Though I might be categorising it too sharply, there were, I believe, six main convictions which dominated the Enlightenment and which have prevailed until the very recent past. They do not belong merely to the ivory tower; they have had an enormous influence on the way all of us have been brought up.

First was the *belief in man*. After the centuries of war and religious persecution which had disfigured Europe, the very idea of God was distasteful to many thinking people by the end of the eighteenth century. Christianity was disgraced. It had not united humankind, but had torn it apart. Reason, not revelation, was clearly the way to go. Man, not God, was the one to rely on. Man controls this world, and our reason enables us to understand how that world works. Who can deny the power of human reason? It has conquered so many diseases and produced our immensely sophisticated technological society. No wonder the atheistic optimists at the end of the eighteenth century erected a statue to the Goddess Reason in the Cathedral of Notre Dame!

Second was *belief in science*. The natural sciences were just beginning to come into their own, with the revolutionary discoveries of Galileo, Bacon and Newton. Very soon it was apparent what enormous benefits the scientific method held out to human beings. Science was the key to the future. We must decline to believe anything on the basis of tradition, religious authority and the like. Instead we must rely on exact observation of how the world works and what it consists of. Here again, the benefits are incalculable. Few of us would want to be deprived of our TV, our Health Service, our computers. But by concentrating on the practical or 'empirical' matters that science could resolve, the minds of the vast majority of people became closed to other forms of knowledge. So much so that most people nowadays assume that scientific knowledge is the only knowledge worth having, and that what cannot be examined by test-tube or microscope cannot be real. A moment's thought will show, of course, how fallacious this is. It is entirely proper to enquire how a thing works and what it consists of. But equally valid questions are 'What is it for?' and 'What is its value?' Science has no answers to such questions, nor does it seek to have. And because of over-concentration on the scientific method, these issues became progressively banished from the public arena. They belonged to the area of private opinion (on which people could legitimately differ in our plural society) rather than public fact (which everyone must accept). The writings of Dr Lesslie Newbigin in our own day have shown what a disaster this chasm between public fact and private opinion has been. He points out that man's evolutionary origins are taught as fact in all our schools, but that there is no agreement and no teaching about what man's destiny is. And that is every bit as important!

A third great pillar of the Enlightenment was closely linked to this infatuation with the scientific method. It was *belief in facts* as opposed to values. Seeing is believing. What you can measure or prove is what matters, and nothing else matters very much. It is consigned to the private realm of values. And on values you are welcome to have your own views, so long as they do not affect other people. Values are your own thing; so is religion. Facts can be proved. Values – and religion – cannot. It does not matter what values or religious convictions people have in their private lives, but woe betide them if these ideas invade the public square of education, politics or commerce!

Fourth, the Enlightenment had a strong *belief in freedom*. Freedom from authority and empire (which were heady goals at a time when the American colonies were kicking out the British, and the French were executing their king and aristocracy). Freedom from the church and its repressive dogmas. Freedom to worship or not as one pleased. Freedom from Christianity as a dominating creed. It was replaced by a rational religion, with one God demanded by reason and an ethics based on utilitarianism; that is to say moral action that worked for the greatest good of the greatest number. It all looked so attractive. 'Liberty, equality, fraternity' – the cry of the French Revolution – characterised the whole Enlightenment outlook. At least that was the theory.

Naturally, in the light of all these convictions, the modern outlook was confident of its *belief in progress*. A better world was on the way, with improved education, relationships and standards of living. This worship of progress was enhanced when Darwin came up with his theory of evolution. It was greeted with enthusiasm across the intellectual spectrum, and was applied not just to biology but to morals, sociology and religion. All climbed enthusiastically on board the train of progress, speeding towards omega point.

Finally, the modernism coined at the Enlightenment was confident of the *belief that human beings are basically good*. To be sure, they may often act badly, but that is because they know no better or because their social conditions are so appalling. Granted good education and good living conditions, we would soon have a notably good society because, in contrast to the Christian belief in universal sinfulness, modernism maintained that we all have a heart of gold. Matters of right and wrong are obvious to all, and mankind would always be rational enough to choose right.

Those were the main convictions of the past 200 years in Europe. Facts were brought to bear against faith. There was much discussion of cause and effect, but little about meaning and destiny. There was much about the individual, but little about community (which was seen as a jungle of individuals where everyone contended for their rights, and were held together, hopefully, by some form of social contract). These two centuries had much to say about know-how, but little about values. Much about man, but nothing about God. Some areas of knowledge were in sharp focus; others in deep shadow.

Today all six pillars of the Age of Reason have been seriously undermined. Despite all that has been delivered by Enlightenment thought and science, it is a worldview which has outlasted its shelf-life. Its arrogant optimism, based on human reason and omnicompetence, looks increasingly pathetic. We are destroying our environment: the rain forests are being hacked down, the seas are becoming fouled up, the air is becoming toxic, the ozone layer is being dissolved, and the effects of nuclear fission and disposal remain a massive threat to the future of mankind. Is this progress? Is it rational?

For the first time in human history mankind has the potential to destroy the whole world many times over by the stockpiles of nuclear weapons spread around an ever-increasing club of cosmic poker players. Is there any reason to suppose that our moral stature has grown at the same pace as our technical ability? The genie of planetary nuclear destruction has been unleashed, and it can never be put back into the bottle.

We have the twin problems of massive population explosion and of terrifying food crisis. Millions starve each year. The poor South and the rich North are on a collision course which cannot be indefinitely delayed.

The threat of our science and technology, unleashed without restraint, cannot be exaggerated. Children can now be born without recourse to a womb, indeed without intercourse taking place at all. Personality can be transformed by the doctors. Not just sheep, but human beings enter the cloning arena. At the same time we see the horrific growth of biological and chemical weapons, defoliants such as devastated Vietnam, and nerve gases like sarin and VR-55. We had a taste of those in the Gulf War. Clearly there is worse to come.

Then think of our diseases. Britain's Health Service is under ever-increasing financial pressure, pressure which will only get worse. Cancer remains as threatening as ever. Mosquitoes are becoming immune to our antitoxins. AIDS is the most potent scourge since the Black Death. But will we change our hedonistic lifestyle? Certainly not. We will continue to fornicate as we please – and put our faith in fallible condoms. And there is always abortion as a last-ditch form of birth control.

We still talk about world peace, but we see little of that brotherhood of man which was the proud boast of the Enlightenment. The United Nations is impotent when it comes to the crunch: think of Rwanda or Bosnia. This century has seen more martyrs for Christianity than all the other centuries put together. This is the century when Stalin slaughtered 50 million of his own Russian compatriots in one way or another, and when the Nazis liquidated 6 million Jews in death camps simply because they were Jews. And in our cities all over the world we see the increase of violence, sadistic murders even by small children, and a complete absence of restraint. The question is: how can we manage to live together? How can man survive?

And as for freedom, it was Rousseau who observed that he saw men claiming to be free, but everywhere in chains. The chains of bigotry, racism, alcoholism, drug addiction, ignorance and prejudice show no signs of being broken. Instead, their grip increases. It is suffocating us.

In the light of all this, the hopes of modernism seem very fragile and unsatisfactory. Where is that freedom, that progress they expected? Has not science, in which they trusted, become the biggest threat to life itself? Who can trust human reason, when marriages collapse, foetuses are scrapped, and nations have been embroiled in more than eighty wars since the end of World War Two, which was supposedly the war to end all wars? Who can believe any longer that human nature is basically good? At best it is a volatile and dangerous mix of good and evil.

In the light of all this the modern worldview has very largely collapsed. It is not the Christians who have caused its downfall. It is the state of the world, the horrors of two world wars, and the destruction of our environment which have shown thinking people that the modern understanding of life was ludicrously optimistic.

The essence of the Enlightenment worldview was that there is some single principle which makes sense of all life. Since God, who had traditionally occupied that role, was out of fashion, reason had been promoted to take his place. But reason has failed to deliver. It is no longer convincing. It never was. Nobody gets married, for instance, on grounds of reason alone! And the three intellectual giants of the last century, Freud, Darwin and Marx, had all made it abundantly clear that human beings do not for the most part act on grounds of reason alone. Freud showed that a lot of what we do is determined by psychological forces. Marx showed that economic forces are decisive in much of our lives. And Darwin showed that evolutionary forces are a major factor in our world. Reason plays a part in none of these.

If God will not do as the cement in our world, and if reason will not do either, what are we left with? The answer, sombre and stark in the extreme, is that nothing is left. There is no cement. There is no longer any 'meta-story', as they say; no great story which makes sense of the world and our place in it. No big story, just a mosaic of little stories, yours and mine among them.

Post-modernism

This cultural revolution called post-modernism, which began to bite in the 1960s, is now everywhere around us. It shouts at us in the TV adverts, where a series of disconnected images in swift succession invites us to buy a particular product. It is not reasoned persuasion – that is old hat nowadays. It is all about feelings, making you feel you need it and want it and must have it. The Age of Reason has been followed by the Age of Feeling. The important thing is to feel good.

Post-modernism is a strange name, indicating that while people know what it comes after, they are not at all sure what it is. It is as hard to define as it is to catch a bar of soap in the bath. But some of the main characteristics are as follows, and it will soon become apparent how hospitable they are to the approach of the Alpha course.

One major characteristic of the post-modern generation is *a quest for meaning and purpose in life*. Many of them do not think there is one, but they long for it all the same. How can you be a fulfilled human being if you have no clear understanding of the purpose of life? 'What is it all about?' asked twenty-three-year-old Carter Cooper as he jumped to his death from his mother's flat in Manhattan. Son of Gloria Vanderbilt, he had every advantage in life. He was young, rich, successful, but had nothing to live for. Bono, of U2 fame, made much the same point when he asked, 'How can you be spokesman for a generation if you've got nothing to say except "Help"?' A few years earlier Albert Camus, whose existentialism was one of the main precursors of post-modernism, observed, 'It is pathetic to see the meaning in life dissipating.'

In this situation where people are crying out for meaning and purpose in life, whether they are aware of it or not, Alpha and its message are enormously attractive. What if there is good news after all? What if there is a living God who is prepared to enlist us in his service and make us his commando troops against the decline and sleaze all around us? Isn't that a purpose which gives meaning to every side of life?

Another poignant aspect of post-modern life is *aloneness*. I say aloneness rather than loneliness, because this is a profound sensation of alienation and can be experienced in a crowd, even at a party. It is always there, and it is too deep for words. In terms of experience it springs from sharing in a culture where people are repeatedly let down, abused and marginalised. Sociologically it is all part of the breakdown of our society, and the collapse of trust in the face of constant disappointment. Aloneness becomes a way of life when relationships have been as savaged as they have in our day. You reject and you are being rejected all the time. As Douglas Coupland, one of the leading spokesmen for the post-modern generation, writes in *Shampoo Planet,* 'I think I know a person and then poof! I find I only know a cartoon version – unknowable and just as lonely and lost as I am, and equally unable to remember that every soul in the world is hurting, not just themselves. It leads to putting on a great mask of being able to cope on the outside, but inside there is terrible emptiness.'

No wonder Alpha speaks so attractively into this situation. It offers community. A community which embraces the whole group. A community based on openness, on the willingness to face any questions without professing to know all the answers. It is a community based on food and enjoyment, humour and the growing appreciation of one another in the light of the dawning belief that we might, after all, be creatures of the living God who has shown something of himself in everyone. Christian fellowship, particularly such as one finds in an Alpha course, is one of the few places where all types and classes, ages and colours discover they can be bound together in mutual acceptance, love and laughter. And those who have for years carried around with them the spectre of a deep inner loneliness, begin to find that they can trust again, and that on the whole their trust is justified. We are not orphans in a land of no tomorrows. We are children in a heavenly Father's family.

Post-modern people are very *suspicious of authority figures*. The royals, the judiciary, the police, schoolteachers and clergy have all come in for a lot of disenchantment and scorn in recent years. Nobody will listen to views which derive from some 'authority' figure or institution any more. They will not be impressed by pomp and circumstance, or by anyone else telling them what to think or do. That is one reason why people hate being preached to. They think (wrongly, as it happens!) that preaching is one person having the cheek to tell them what to do. 'Get lost!' they say. 'I'm going to do my own thing.'

It is the age of doing your own thing. And that is precisely where the Alpha course is so helpful. It is not based on authority. It does not come from a pulpit. It is not a truth claim from six feet above contradiction, but an explanation of what, if it is true, is the most marvellous thing in the world. And all this takes place in the company of fellow seekers, gathered in ongoing exploration round a meal. What a difference that makes. No wonder Alpha does not work when people decide to dispense with the meal and have weak tea out of green church cups instead! Jesus got his friends together round meals and banquets. That is what Alpha does. And it is very winsome. Moreover the course does not have to be taught by a clergyman. And even if it is, he does not do so on the basis of authority and institution. If you watch a Nicky Gumbel video there is nothing about his dress, manner or content to suggest that he is a race apart, a clergyman. No, he is one of the seekers himself, but one who has had a bit more experience than some, and is willing to offer clues for the journey for people to consider. Above all it is personal exploration at one's own pace that is the key to Alpha's success in this matter of Christian content.

Many post-moderns are very *suspicious of any claims to truth*. They wonder if there can be any such thing, since so much that purports to be truth is nothing of the kind, but a horrible type of propaganda. 'Truth claims are power games,' they say. And that would seem to put Christianity beyond the pale before you start looking at it. For the Christian gospel makes very strong claims to truth. But there is no suggestion of power games in real Christianity. Nobody is attempting to exercise power or persuasion over anyone else. The leaders are simply saying, 'We believe we have found something that is both true and satisfying. Why not have a good look at it and see how it strikes you? Try it for size.' That will not in any way threaten the post-modern, who is interested in people and their stories (remember, there is no big story these days, so all our little stories gain extra significance). If you have found something in it, your friend is also likely to find it well worth investigating – so long as he likes and trusts you. And because nobody is forcing him to accept something on the basis of tradition, authority or superiority, but on the level – why, he is willing to give it a go.

Post-modern people are often *perplexed about personal identity* in this impersonal age when you are as often a number as a person. This is a day of massive self-absorption and self-questioning. People are intensely concerned about their image – the reality can look after itself!

This preoccupation is born of a lack of self-confidence in a world that seems to be falling apart. It is the result of deep insecurity, and you find it everywhere. Three of the most important questions that are rarely asked but often thought about are: Who am I? What am I worth? and Where am I headed?

Here again Alpha is wonderfully reassuring. It asserts both by its teaching and by its companionship centred in Christ that we are not just a bunch of chemicals in suspension; not merely a grown-up collection of genes. That is to rubbish our humanity. No, we are far more than that. We are made in the image of God. We are special. We are worth so much to God that he has come to find us, and indeed to die on a ghastly cross in order to woo us back to the God we have rejected and perhaps sworn did not exist. And he cares about us so much that when we die we do not go out like a light, but we go to spend eternity with him who gave us life in the first place. If that is true, if it even *might* be true, it gives a totally new sense of self-worth. I matter to God so much that he made me in his image, he ransomed me from my foolish rebellion and self-induced alienation, and he wants to have me with him for ever. Wow! That is not dull religion. It is life. And Jesus maintained, 'I have come that they may have life, and have it to the full' (John 10:10).

Post-moderns are *looking for reality*. They are fed up with the hype of politicians, preachers and advertisers. They are streetwise. They are not easily conned. Unlike previous protest generations who enthusiastically chose their way of life, post-moderns are reluctant rebels. They simply see no alternative to fragmentation and alienation since there is no big story to believe in, no principle of coherence in a crazy world. They see no way out, but desperately long for one. But they will not be easily won over to anything. They will not be taken in by hype or cliché, least of all by a Christian hard sell.

But that is, once again, where Alpha scores. It is not hard sell. It is fun. It is humorous. It is social. It is food-centred. And being in the same group with a good many Christians over some three months gives an excellent opportunity to see if they are real or not. I recall that when I first heard the wonder of the Christian message in my middle teens I was equally determined not to be taken in. I watched those who professed this vital faith to see if it made any difference to the way they lived their daily lives. After a few months I was certain that it did. These people had something I did not. And I wanted it badly. That began my change from a seeker to a finder. The integrity of Christian lifestyle is a vital part of the appeal of Alpha. And the length of the course means that you are inevitably driven to have a good long look at the integrity and reality of the experience claimed by others.

The post-modern generation is very *short on hope*. Few people today think the world is becoming a better place. Few think things will be easier for their generation than it was for their parents. Gone is the evolutionary optimism of the old days. Nobody talks any more about the inevitability of progress. Many feel there is not a lot to look forward to in a world riddled with war, AIDS and unemployment. Indeed, one of the main reasons why young post-moderns today are so set on instant gratification is because the past has nothing to teach them (it belonged to the bad old days of modernism) and the future does not bear thinking about. The present is all you are left with. It is a *now* generation, seeking instant satisfaction, because there is no knowing what disasters tomorrow will bring.

What a difference the Christian gospel makes to this

attitude, especially when it is given solid embodiment in a group of people bound together by a common search and experience. The heart of the gospel is all about hope. It concerns the future which the crucified Jesus has opened up for all who will accept him. And this is no pie in the sky. It is solidly grounded in history. A cross you could get splinters from if you rubbed your hand against it. A tomb, an empty tomb, you could graze your foot on if you were not careful. Christians are not whistling in the wind to keep their spirits up when they talk about heaven. Our confidence is founded on the solid fact that death has been beaten by this Jesus. He is alive for evermore. History is not 'a tale told by an idiot, full of sound and fury, signifying nothing', as Shakespeare has it. History is *his* story, with a start, a mid-point (when its Author came upon our stage – a date we set our calendars by) and a future glorious consummation. The events of the mid-point are the clue to the nature of the outcome. It was like that in World War Two, when the events of D-day pointed inexorably towards the outcome on V-Day, despite the long months of battle and indeed reverses which lay in between. An Alpha group is a community of hope, experiencing in the here and now a foretaste of God's future. And that is a marvellous antidote to hopelessness.

A final characteristic to which I want to draw attention is at first sight rather surprising. But today's post-modern generation is *hungry for spiritual experience*. They have seen the emptiness of materialism and rationalism. To be sure, they want their material goodies, but they know that these do not provide inner satisfaction. They have only to look to their parents' generation to see that. They are impatient of rational argument (and if we Christians rely on that alone, we are doomed to fail). They care nothing about tradition and institutions. They want life and experience for themselves. People say this is a materialistic age. That is only partly true. It is an age of intense spiritual questing. You see it in the new therapies which abound. You see it in the cults which multiply at an amazing rate. You see it in the fascination of *Star Wars* and the like, longing for a rescue from beyond ourselves. You see it, above all, in the remarkable growth of the New Age spirituality. The New Age, though thoroughly incoherent and probably short-lived, shows today's hunger for something bigger than our own little selves. It shows an openness to spiritual experimentation and celebration. It shows a strong reaction against the mindless accumulation of material possessions, as though these could give satisfaction to empty hearts. The cults, the paranormal, the alternative medicine, the crystals, the exuberant and worldwide expression of grief when Princess Diana was killed – all these show a profound spiritual hunger. Not that people are flocking into the churches. They are not, on the whole. They probably feel the church is too much bound by institutional life, dogma and hierarchy to have much to say to them. They do not feel that we in the church have the spirituality they are looking for. Or maybe if they do, they fear that it comes at too high a cost in discipleship and morals.

But what a powerful impact an Alpha course can have! Here is a group of people who are hungry for experience. They are determined to find out if this Christian thing is real and how they can get involved in it, if it is. They see some rays of a Christlike spirituality shining out from some of the members and leaders of the course who are already Christians, and this spurs their quest. For in Alpha, people can find a spirituality which does not, like the New Age, rubbish our reason. Here is a worship which has informality and silence, joyful praise, good engagement with Scripture, intelligent questions and answers, and personal testimony to God's reality from members of the group. A powerful mixture, and a very attractive introduction to authentic spirituality.

Something for everyone

These seem to me to be the main reasons why Alpha has made such a hit at this particular time. Of course, not everyone is post-modern. But as my friend James Lawrence acutely points out, there are other important reasons for its fruitfulness. People encounter Christ in a variety of ways. For some it is *exposure* to a reality they had never even dreamed of, supremely the reality of the Holy Spirit. For others the hunger for spiritual *experience* leads them to Alpha. Others value clear, no-nonsense *explanations*. Solid *evidence* is crucial to many people, while others relish *exploring* things for themselves. It is at once obvious that all these different approaches are catered for in Alpha.

Some people are bowled over by the fact that so many folk are keen to eat together and discuss God with enthusiasm. In due course many of them find themselves exposed to the reality of Jesus and his life-giving Spirit. Many others these days are engaged on a spiritual search, and find the partnership of the group on this journey particularly valuable, especially in the pleasant surroundings of the meal. Others value clear teaching – explanation which makes sense and is based on solid evidence. There is plenty of both in the talk and the book for people like that. But those who prefer to make their own exploration have every opportunity to do so in Alpha, through the questions they ask, the material they study and the discussions they engage in. It is part of the genius of the course that there is, in the varied experiences of the evening, something which meets the particular concerns of almost all types of people.

All personality types

Many people these days are familiar with the Myers-Briggs analysis of personality types. This suggests that people use two 'perceiving functions' in order to collect information on which they will make decisions. Naturally people use both, but they tend to have an overriding preference for one.

Thus some who have a preference for 'sensing' (S) will primarily respond to facts. They are likely to be attracted by practical reasons for belief and the difference it makes. They like a systematic approach, and are inclined to ask the 'how' and 'why' questions. Well, the teaching, the questions and the systematic approach of Alpha will appeal to them.

Then there are those who have a preference for 'intuition' (N), and respond best to challenges to their imagination, to arresting ideas and exciting possibilities. Alpha is ideal for them, with its spiritual encounter, its opportunity to exchange ideas and come face to face with the ideal which Jesus and his gospel presents, particularly the vision and the possibilities for future change which it holds out.

Others may prefer to use 'feeling' (F) first, and are strong on issues of the heart and the stuff of human relationships. They are likely to be drawn by the sheer love of God as they get involved in Alpha, and to be moved by the possibility of a personal relationship with him.

Then there are those who tend to prefer thinking (the Ts). They may want to work out the logic of a position and make decisions based on that. It is truth issues that are particularly important for them. And that is exactly what the careful and systematic teaching of Alpha, backed up with solid evidence, is calculated to address.

The Myers-Briggs Personality Type Indicator also detects two main ways in which people like to run their lives. There are those with a preference for 'judgement' (the Js), who are generally good at making decisions and sticking to them. They will probably be attracted by the evidence laid out in the Alpha course which calls for decision. And then there are the Ps, the people who prefer 'perception', and are by nature inquisitive. They tend to keep open minds and revisit decisions in the light of new information. They may well be drawn into an Alpha by sheer curiosity, and may be willing in the light of what they encounter there to change their minds and get involved in real Christianity.

Moreover, most of us are inclined towards either extroversion or introversion; that is to say, we get our main source of personal renewal either from being out with other people, or from being apart. The extrovert usually wants to talk things out, and is happy in a large group. There is no problem about that in Alpha! The introvert, on the other hand, will probably prefer to think a thing through carefully before talking about it, and certainly before making a decision. Well, the length of the course, and the opportunity for developing genuine friendships within it, appeals to them. They can sit quietly and observe if they like. Nobody is pressing them for any decision; they have every opportunity to take their time. Alpha, therefore, has attraction for introverts as well as extroverts.

So long as nobody wants to harden these preferences into watertight compartments they can be a helpful way of looking at the God-given stuff of our basic personalities. They may well go some distance towards explaining the almost universal appeal of this course. But you can never put the Almighty in a box. God through his Holy Spirit often reaches people through their least preferred functions! The main point is that Alpha provides a highly acceptable milieu for people of very different temperaments and outlooks.

Naturally there are other reasons for the success of Alpha. It is superbly produced, packaged and marketed. Its very success breeds success. The videos, books and other teaching materials are first class. The training course is invaluable. But above all, Alpha speaks to today's generation because it engages both with the Scriptures and the culture of the day. Those are the two terminals through which the current flows so powerfully.

For more information on Alpha contact the Alpha office, Holy Trinity Brompton, on 0207 581 8255 or visit the website at www.alpha.org.uk.

Alpha titles by Nicky Gumbel, published by Kingsway Publications unless otherwise noted.

Why Jesus? A booklet – given to all participants at the start of the Alpha course. (Available from Holy Trinity Brompton.)

'The clearest, best illustrated and most challenging short presentation of Jesus that I know.' – Michael Green

Why Christmas? The Christmas version of *Why Jesus?* (Available from Holy Trinity Brompton.)

Questions of Life The Alpha course in book form. In fifteen compelling chapters Nicky Gumbel points the way to an authentic Christianity which is exciting and relevant to today's world.

Searching Issues The seven issues most often raised by participants on the Alpha course: suffering, other religions, sex before marriage, the New Age, homosexuality, science and Christianity, and the Trinity.

A Life Worth Living Based on the book of Philippians, this is an invaluable next step for those who have just completed the Alpha course, and for anyone eager to put their faith on a firm biblical footing.

Telling Others: The Alpha Initiative The theological principles and the practical details of how courses are run. Each alternate chapter consists of a testimony of someone whose life has been changed by God through an Alpha course.

Challenging Lifestyle Studies in the Sermon on the Mount showing how Jesus' teaching flies in the face of modern lifestyle and presents us with a radical alternative.

The Heart of Revival Interpreting some of the teaching in Isaiah, Nicky Gumbel draws out important truths for today's church to give you not only a fresh hunger and expectation for revival but also a proper understanding of what it might mean and how we can prepare.